James Alexander McClymont

The New Testament and Its Writers

James Alexander McClymont

The New Testament and Its Writers

ISBN/EAN: 9783337385859

Printed in Europe, USA, Canada, Australia, Japan

Cover: Foto ©Lupo / pixelio.de

More available books at **www.hansebooks.com**

THE NEW TESTAMENT

AND

ITS WRITERS

BY THE

REV. J. A. M'CLYMONT, D.D. (EDIN.)

JOINT-TRANSLATOR OF DR. J. T. BECK'S 'PASTORAL THEOLOGY OF
THE NEW TESTAMENT,' AND AUTHOR OF THE COMMENTARY
ON ST. JOHN'S GOSPEL IN THE 'CENTURY BIBLE'

THIRTY-NINTH THOUSAND
NEW EDITION, REVISED AND ENLARGED

LONDON: A. & C. BLACK: SOHO SQUARE
EDINBURGH: R. & R. CLARK, LIMITED
PUBLICATION AGENTS FOR THE CHURCH OF SCOTLAND

1902

AUTHOR'S PREFACE

THE author is glad to know that in addition to its circulation as a Bible-Class text-book, *The New Testament and its Writers* has been of service to many adult students who desire to learn something for themselves of the authenticity and original purpose of the various writings of which the Sacred Record is composed. It is for such general readers that the present edition is chiefly intended. The text has been carefully revised ; the chapter on *Galatians* has been recast in the light of recent discussions ; and the additional matter introduced in the form of Notes and Appendix will, it is hoped, considerably enhance the value of the book for those whose library does not contain many works of a Biblical nature.

For information on a number of kindred topics (such as the Canon, MSS., Versions, Textual Criticism) and for fuller notes, the reader may be referred to the demy 8vo edition of this book recently published.

J. A. M'CLYMONT.

NOTE

In Scripture References, when the name of the Book is not given, the citations refer to the Book under discussion.

When Scripture is quoted, the words of the Revised Version are given.

R.V. = Revised Version.

A.V. = Authorised Version.

MS. = Manuscript.

Cf. = Compare.

CONTENTS

APPENDIX A

APPENDIX B

THE NEW TESTAMENT AND ITS WRITERS

CHAPTER I

THE NEW TESTAMENT

1. Name.—The New Testament forms the second and concluding portion of the Revelation given to the world in the line of Jewish history. It derives its name from an expression used by the Lord Jesus Christ in the institution of the rite which was designed to commemorate His death—"This cup is the new testament in my blood"—more correctly, "This cup is the new covenant in my blood" (R.V.), in contrast with the old covenant made with Moses (Luke xxii. 20; Matt. xxvi. 28; 1 Cor. xi. 25; cf. Exod. xxiv. 8). The use of the word "testament" in this sense was due to the Latin *testamentum*, which was early adopted as an equivalent for the Greek word meaning "covenant."

2. Language.—A period of about four hundred years had elapsed after the last of the Old Testament Scriptures was written before the New Testament was commenced. In the interval the Jewish people, spreading far and wide in the pursuit of arts and commerce, had become familiar

with the Greek tongue, which was the intellectual bond
of the civilised world, as the Roman empire was its bond
in a social and political sense.   Into this language the
Scriptures of the Old Testament had been translated from
the Hebrew, about 200 B.C., at Alexandria, the great
meeting-place of Rabbinical learning and Hellenic culture.[1]   From the amalgamation of these and other
elements there resulted a form of Greek known as the
"common" or Hellenistic Greek. · It was in this language that the New Testament was written—a language
marvellously fitted for the purpose, both because of the
wide prevalence of Greek among the civilised nations of
the time (resulting from the conquests of Alexander
the Great), and on account of its unrivalled clearness,
richness, and flexibility.   Hence the New Testament
has been aptly described as having "a Greek body, a
Hebrew soul, and a Christian spirit that animates them
both."[2]

3. Contents.—The New Testament Scriptures consist
of twenty-seven different books, varying in their form
and character—the first in order mainly historical, the
next doctrinal, and the concluding portion relating to
vision and prophecy.   This is an order somewhat analogous to that found in the Old Testament, many of whose
characteristics alike as regards thought and expression
are reflected in the New Testament.   The twenty-seven
books are the work of nine different authors (assuming
the Epistle to the Hebrews to have been written by some
other person than St. Paul), each book having its special
characteristics corresponding to the personality of its
writer and the circumstances in which it was written, but

---

[1] The Septuagint, so called because said to have been executed by
seventy Jews brought to Alexandria from Jerusalem for this purpose
by Ptolemy Philadelphus.   The work was done very gradually and
with varying degrees of skill between 280 B.C. and 150 B.C.

[2] Dr. Ph. Schaff, *Hist. Ap. Ch.* p. 573.

all forming part of one divine whole [1] centred in the Lord
Jesus Christ and essentially related to an unseen world.
They were written at various times, but all in the latter
half of the first century [2]—except perhaps the Epistle of
James, which was probably written before 50 A.D.

4. **Manuscripts.**—The original MSS. have all perished.
If written on papyrus for ordinary use, they would not
last,[3] while those of a more durable substance would be
in frequent danger of destruction at the hands of persecutors.[4] Hence the vast majority of extant MSS. are
of a comparatively modern date—anterior, however, to
the invention of printing in 1450, when the copying of
MSS. practically ceased. A few precious copies written
on vellum or parchment have come down to us from a
very early period, the most important of which are (1)
the Sinaitic (Codex ℵ), discovered by Tischendorf in St.
Catherine's Convent at the foot of Mount Sinai in 1859,
now deposited at St. Petersburg, dating from the fourth
century ; (2) the Vatican, styled Codex B, preserved in the
Vatican Library at Rome, likewise of the fourth century ;

---

[1] "The books of Scripture are a series, not a congeries. This is
true of the Bible as a whole, and is the most remarkable fact in
literature as well as in religion."—Prof. Charteris, *The New Testament
Scriptures*, p. 3.

[2] Speaking generally, this may now be said to be the opinion of the
great majority of critics who are willing to be guided by evidence as
they would in the case of any other books. "In recent years," says
Prof. Ramsay in his preface to *The Church in the Roman Empire*,
"as I came to understand Roman history better, I have realised that,
in the case of almost all the books in the New Testament, it is as gross
an outrage on criticism to hold them for second century forgeries as it
would be to class the works of Horace and Virgil as forgeries of the
time of Nero."

[3] The Egyptian and other papyri to be found in museums owe their
preservation to special circumstances which saved them from exposure
and from tear and wear.

[4] For example, immense numbers of MSS. were destroyed by
Imperial edict in the Diocletian persecution in the beginning of the
fourth century : and even in Britain (as we learn from Gildas the
historian) great piles were burned during the persecutions of the third
century.

(3) the Alexandrine (Codex A), preserved in the British Museum, and dating from the fifth century; (4) Codex Ephraemi (C), also of the fifth century—a *palimpsest*, the original writing having been effaced in the twelfth century (but now revived) to make room for the writings of Ephraem Syrus; and (5) Codex Bezæ (D), of the sixth century, preserved in the University Library of Cambridge.   These and other ancient MSS. to the number of about a hundred are called Uncials, because written with capital letters without any separation between the words, —the others of a more modern character being called Minuscules or Cursives, because written in a small running hand.   Of the latter there are about 2000—an immense array of witnesses compared with the few MSS. of classical works preserved to us, which can frequently be counted on the ten fingers.   Owing to the greater liability to error in copying with the hand than in the use of the printing press, about 200,000 Various Readings have been discovered in the extant MSS. of the New Testament.   Happily the differences between the readings are for the most part so minute that they do not affect the substance of revealed truth.   As it is the duty of the Church, however, to ascertain, as far as possible, the exact words of the sacred writers, a special department of study has been instituted, commonly known as Textual Criticism, which has for its aim to adjudicate on the rival claims of the various readings, with due regard to the age and special characteristics of the several manuscripts, as well as to the common risks of misapprehension and inadvertence to which all copyists were liable.

5. **Other Witnesses.**—In the performance of the difficult and delicate task just mentioned attention must be paid to two other valuable sources of information. (1) Those writings of Church Fathers—ranging from the end of the first century to the fourth or fifth century of the

Christian era—which contain quotations from the New Testament.[1] The value of the Fathers as a help in determining the exact text of Scripture is a good deal impaired by the fact that, not having the advantage of a Concordance, or of our divisions into chapters and verses, they frequently quote from memory and not with strict accuracy.[2] This is of less moment, however, when the object is not so much to ascertain the precise language of Scripture as to prove the existence and general reception of the books of the New Testament at an early period in the history of the Church.[3] (2) Ancient Versions or Translations, some of which (for example the Syriac and Old Latin) were made within a century after the time of the apostles.[4]

6. **English Versions.**—The first English Version was completed by John Wycliff in 1383. It was, however, only the translation of a translation (the Latin Vulgate

---

[1] In this respect, as well as in the matter of MSS., the New Testament books occupy a much better position than most of the ancient classics.

[2] The first Concordance was produced by Antonius of Padua, followed by Cardinal Hugo, in the thirteenth century. To the latter was also due the division of the Bible into the existing chapters ; but the division into verses was the work of Robert Stephens, the celebrated editor and printer of the New Testament.

[3] For information regarding the Church Fathers whose citations are referred to in subsequent chapters, see Appendix A, pp. 193-202. The citations themselves may be found in Charteris' *Canonicity*, or in Westcott's *History of the New Testament Canon*.

[4] These, also, afford valuable evidence as to the canonicity of particular books—some of them having been current as early as the second century, and being still preserved in ancient MSS. dating, in some cases, from the fourth, fifth, and sixth centuries. As regards *readings*, their testimony is often uncertain owing to the want of exact correspondence between their language and that of the original ; but where the translation is of a literal character, as it is, for example, in the case of the Old Latin Versions, the language of the original in a disputed passage may be inferred with a near approach to certainty. Even the errors of the translator sometimes indicate quite plainly what words he had before him in the Greek ; while, in a question of the omission or insertion of a clause, an ordinary version speaks as plainly as a MS. in the original.

of St. Jerome). The first English translation from the Greek was finished by William Tyndale in 1525, and put in print the following year at Worms. This was followed by Miles Coverdale's translation of the whole Bible in 1535, the *Great Bible*, usually called *Cranmer's* (for use in Churches), in 1539, the *Geneva Bible* in 1557, the *Bishops' Bible* in 1568, and *King James's Bible* (the *Authorised Version*) in 1611. The most recent and reliable results of Biblical criticism are embodied in the Revised Version of 1881, which has in this respect, as in regard to accuracy of translation, an unquestionable superiority over the Authorised Version, the latter having been made at a time when the science was still in its infancy, and before any of the three chief MSS. above mentioned were available for reference. Possibly the next generation may see further improvements, as the result of a closer examination of MSS., Versions, and other ancient writings, as well as through an enhanced appreciation of the language of the New Testament, in the light of the Greek translation of the Old Testament (the Septuagint) and other Hellenistic literature ; but, after all, any points in which our English Bible is capable of improvement are infinitesimal compared with the general trustworthiness of its contents. Of its imperfections as a translation it may be said, with scarcely less truth than of obscurities in the original, that "like the spots upon the surface of the sun, they neither mar the symmetry nor impair the glory of the great Source of our Life and Light which is imaged in them."

CHAPTER II

1. Name and Nature.—At the head of the New Testament stand the four Gospels. This position has been fitly assigned to them, because, although by no means the earliest written of the New Testament Books, they contain a record of the life and ministry of Jesus Christ which forms the corner-stone of the whole fabric— Christianity being essentially a historical religion, basing its doctrines not on fancy but on fact. The name gospel, which is the Saxon equivalent for a word in the original meaning "good tidings," was first of all applied to Christ's preaching (Matt. iv. 23 ; Mark i. 15), and to that of the apostles (1 Cor. ix. 16). In course of time it came to be applied also to the books containing a record of the great facts and truths which formed the substance of that preaching. One of the earliest writers to use the word in this sense is Justin Martyr, who wrote about the middle of the second century.[1] He frequently refers to *Memoirs* composed by the apostles and their companions,

---

[1] Basilides (125 A.D.), quoted by Hippolytus, cites John i. 9 as "said in *the Gospels*," but some think, without much reason, that the words are to be referred to one of Basilides' school merely. Another instance has been found in the *Apology of Aristides*, dating probably from the early part of the second century, which mentions "the sacred writing which among them (the Christians) is called Gospel" (literally "evangelic"), and also in the *Didaché*, which seems even older.

which, as he tells us, were called "Gospels"; and he informs us that they were read along with the writings of the prophets at the meetings for Christian worship on the Lord's Day.

2. **Authenticity.**—That the *Memoirs* to which Justin refers are the same as the Gospels which we now possess may be inferred from the circumstance that almost all the facts concerning Christ's life which he mentions in about 200 scattered passages of his writings are found in one or other of the four Gospels, while in all the express quotations—seven in number—which he makes from the *Memoirs* the words quoted are also to be found in our Gospels. This conclusion is strengthened by the fact that about twenty years later (170 A.D.) a disciple of Justin named Tatian, a well-informed and far-travelled man, drew up in the Syriac language a sort of harmony of the four Gospels (called *Diatessaron*), which had a very large circulation in the East. An Arabic translation of this work and a Syriac commentary on it have recently been discovered, from which it is evident that the four Gospels on which Tatian's work was founded were identical with ours. In the *Muratorian Fragment*, also, there is a list of New Testament books, which most critics assign to about 170 A.D., where the Gospels of Luke and John are mentioned as third and fourth, the other two being apparently mentioned in a part of the MS. now lost. If further corroboration be needed, we have it in the universally-admitted fact that fifteen years later (185 A.D.) the four Gospels which we possess were circulated in all parts of Christendom—Europe, Asia, and Africa—in thousands of copies for the use of innumerable Christians who heard them read at their weekly meetings for worship.

For these reasons it seems to admit of no doubt that Justin Martyr's Gospels were the same as ours; and it is

easy to trace them back through a series of still earlier
writers to the testimony of the apostles. We know that
Marcion the Gnostic [1] (140 A.D.) built his system largely
on the Gospel of Luke, of which he published a mutilated
edition known as Marcion's Luke. In contrast with
Marcion, Tertullian places Valentinus, another Gnostic
(140-160 A.D.), as one who used the canon in its entirety.
A prominent witness is Papias (Bishop of Hierapolis),
who wrote an *Exposition of the Oracles of Our Lord* about
135 A.D., when he was an old man. Among other things
which he had gathered from personal intercourse with
friends of the apostles and with two disciples of the Lord
(one "the Elder John"), he tells us the circumstances
under which Matthew wrote his *Oracles* and Mark his
Oracles of the Lord.[2] Still earlier, we find many quotations more or less exact from our Gospels in the lately-
discovered *Didaché*, or "Teaching of the Twelve
Apostles" (dating from the end of the first or the early
part of the second century), in the language of Basilides
(125 A.D.), who wrote twenty-four books on "the Gospel,"
and in the short extant writings of Polycarp (a disciple of
the Apostle John, who wrote before 115 A.D., martyred
155-156 A.D.), of Hermas and "Barnabas" (early in the
second century), and of Clement of Rome (95-96 A.D.).[3]

[1] The *Gnostics* (who derived their name from a Greek word meaning
knowledge) claimed a deeper insight into the mysteries of religion than
was possessed by the ordinary believer. But they always professed to
be indebted for this knowledge to their fuller comprehension of the
meaning of Scripture. Hence the frequency of their appeals to the
New Testament writings. For the earliest distinct traces in the
Christian Church of the tendencies which afterwards developed into
Gnosticism, see pp. 119, 120 and 180-182.

[2] Cf. pp. 26, 195.

[3] The extant Christian writings of the first century (other than the
New Testament) are extremely meagre, while the writings of the second
century till near its close are mainly defences of Christianity (*Apologies*)
addressed to unbelievers, with fewer quotations from the New Testament than if they had been intended for members of the Church.
But the substance, and even the language, of our Gospels is woven into
the earliest Christian writings that have come down to us.

They are also found in all MSS. of the Syriac and Old Latin Versions, both of which are known to have existed in the second century, the Syriac in the earlier half of it. To this we may add that in the undisputed epistles of Paul, written within a generation after our Lord's death, there are numerous allusions to Christ's history, teaching, and example, which harmonise with the facts recorded in the four Gospels.

In these circumstances we may challenge those who throw doubt on the credibility of the Gospels to show at what period it was even *possible* for forgery or falsification to be perpetrated, and perpetrated so successfully as to impose upon all branches of the Church, leaving its members and teachers utterly unconscious of the deception that had been practised on them—this, too, in matters affecting the most vital interests of the Church's faith, regarding which the apostles had been testifying ever since the day of Pentecost on which they began to preach in the name of their Risen Master.

Of the estimation in which the Gospels were held we may judge from the words of Irenæus, a disciple of Polycarp, who, towards the close of the second century, speaks of the written Gospel as " the foundation and pillar of our faith "; and says regarding the Scriptures— which he defines to be the writings both of prophet and evangelist—" the Scriptures, being spoken by the Word and Spirit of God, are perfect." [1]

3. **Origin.**—For many years, probably for more than a generation, after the death of Christ, there does not appear to have been any authorised record of His life and teaching in the Church. The charge which the apostles

---

[1] The genuineness of the fourth Gospel is specially dealt with in chap. vi., where additional evidence will be found specially applicable to that Gospel.

had received from their Master was to preach the Gospel, and the promise of the Spirit had been expressly connected with the bearing of oral testimony (Matt. x. 19, 20). As they had received nothing in writing from their Master's hands, it was not likely they would see any necessity for a written Word so long as they were able to fulfil their commission to preach the Gospel, especially as they were looking for a speedy return of their Lord, and had no idea that so many centuries were to elapse before the great event should take place. The preaching of the Gospel was enough to tax their energies to the utmost; and the task of committing to writing was not more alien to the customs of their nation than it would be uncongenial to their own habits as uneducated Galileans. Hence we can readily understand how it was that the Old Testament Scriptures, to which the apostles constantly appealed for proof that Jesus was the Messiah, continued to be for many years the only inspired writings acknowledged by the Christian Church. A New Testament in our sense of the term was something which the apostles never dreamt of; and it is not to the design of man, but to the inscrutable influence of the divine Spirit and the overruling working of divine Providence, that we owe the composition of our Gospels before the apostles and other eye-witnesses of the Saviour's ministry had passed away. Drawn up without concert and without the formal sanction of the Church, they contain in a simple form, suitable for all ages and for all classes, several independent records of Christ's life and teaching, of which it may be said with truth that they are better authenticated and more nearly contemporaneous with the events than almost any other record we possess in connection with any period of ancient history. Their dignity and truthfulness are only rendered the more conspicuous when they are contrasted with the apocryphal gospels invented at a later period, which were designed not so much to meet the spiritual wants of the Church as to gratify an idle curiosity.[1]

It is a remarkable fact that two of our Gospels do not claim to have been written by apostles, but only by companions of apostles (Mark and Luke); and that of the other two only one bears the name of an apostle of eminence (John). This is, so far, a confirmation of their genuineness; for if they had been forgeries claiming an authority to which they were not entitled, they would have been pretty sure to claim it in the highest form. The same circumstance shows that the apostles generally did not regard it as a duty to record their testimony in writing.

In the discharge of their commission as preachers of the Gospel, they doubtless followed the practice which was common in the East of trusting to memory rather than to written documents; and as the Church extended, and they were no longer able to minister personally to the wants of their converts or of those who required to have the Gospel preached to them, it would become their duty to train evangelists and catechists to assist them in the work. In preaching to the heathen, it would only be the leading facts of Christ's life that would require to be proclaimed, but in the instruction of those who had already accepted the message of salvation it would be necessary to go more into detail, and set Christ before them as a guide and pattern in their daily life. This instruction was doubtless given in an oral form, the

---

[1] About fifty apocryphal Gospels are known to us (besides Acts, Epistles, and Apocalypses); but of many only the names or brief fragments have been preserved. They usually abounded in the strange and marvellous, more especially in connection with the infancy and childhood of our Lord; and traces of their influence may be seen in Christian art and poetry. To support some heresy was the purpose of many of the apocryphal Gospels.

scholars repeating the lesson again and again after their teachers.[1]

The history of Christ's life and teaching was thus originally set forth not in the form of a chronological narrative but rather as a series of lessons imparted by the apostles and their fellow-labourers as occasion required, or "to meet the needs of their hearers," as one of the early Church Fathers (Papias) says, referring to Peter's style of preaching. During the twelve years or more that elapsed before the dispersion of the apostles from Jerusalem, a recognised course of instruction had doubtless gained currency in the Church, corresponding to St. Peter's definition of the period in the life of Christ which was the proper subject for apostolic testimony— "Beginning from the baptism of John unto the day that he (Jesus) was received up from us" (Acts i. 22). With this agree specimens of apostolic preaching contained in the Book of Acts (iv. 19, 20; x. 36-43; xiii. 23-31), as well as allusions which the apostles make in their epistles to the Gospel preached by them, and to the knowledge of Christ's life acquired by their converts (1 Cor. ii. 2; xi. 23-27; xv. 1-4; Gal. iii. 1; 1 Pet. i. 18-21, etc.) A close examination of such passages makes it evident that, while Christ Jesus was the constant theme of the apostles' preaching, they dwelt chiefly on the great facts that formed the consummation of His ministry—His sufferings, death, and resurrection; and we may regard it as an evidence of the faithfulness with which our Gospels represent the earliest preaching and teaching of the apostles, that they give such prominence to the closing scenes in our Lord's history. We have another token of

---

[1] This is the meaning of the word "instructed" (literally *catechised*) in Luke i. 4. We have another trace of such systematic instruction in the expression used in Acts ii. 42: "They" (the converts) "continued stedfastly in the apostles' teaching."

their authenticity in the fact that they narrate events not in the light reflected on them by the subsequent teaching of the Spirit, but as they were actually regarded by the disciples at the time of their occurrence.

It would seem that before our Gospels were composed, attempts had been made by private persons to draw up a connected history of the Saviour's life, or at least of His ministry. Such attempts are referred to by St. Luke in the preface to his Gospel (i. 1-4). In all probability he is alluding to other documents than the Gospels we possess, not only because he speaks of the writers as "many," in a tone scarcely consistent with the respect due to apostolic authors, but because a comparison of the four Gospels leads to the conclusion that he could not have had any of the three others before him when he drew up his narrative. Whatever part the documents referred to by St. Luke may have had in determining the shape in which the oral Gospel was finally to be recorded, all of them were ultimately superseded by our present Gospels, in whose preservation and triumph we may see an illustration, in the highest sense, of "the survival of the fittest."

4. Diversity.—On a comparison of the several Gospels, a marked difference is at once apparent between the fourth and the three preceding ones. The latter are called *synoptical*, because they give in one common view the same general outline of the ministry of Christ. This outline is almost entirely confined to His ministry in Galilee and includes only one visit to Jerusalem ; whereas the fourth Gospel gives an account of no less than five visits to the capital, and lays the scene of the ministry chiefly in Judæa. A still more important distinction between them, with regard to the nature of their contents, has been briefly expressed by designating the synoptical Gospels as the *bodily* Gospels, and St. John's as the *spiritual* Gospel—by which it is meant that the former relate chiefly to outward events connected with the Saviour's visible presence, reported for the most part without note or comment, while the latter is designed to represent the ideal and heavenly side of His personality and work. Akin to this distinction is the fact that the first three Gospels report Christ's addresses to the multitude, consisting largely of parables, while the fourth Gospel contains discourses of a more sublime character, frequently expressed in the language of allegory and addressed to the inner circle of His followers.

When we enter into a closer examination of the three synoptic Gospels and compare them with one another, we find an amount of similarity in detail, extending even to minute expressions and the connection of individual incidents, combined with a diversity of diction, arrangement, and contents, which it has hitherto baffled the ingenuity of critics to explain fully. A general idea of their mutual relations may be gathered from the following comparison. If the contents of each Gospel be reckoned 100, the relative proportion of those things in which a Gospel agrees with one or other of its fellows to those things in which it stands alone would be as follows :—

	Peculiarities.	Coincidences.
St. Matthew	42	58
St. Mark	7	93
St. Luke	59	41

It is found that the coincidences in *language* are much fewer than they are in *substance*—which is only what might have been expected, if the several accounts are derived from independent witnesses. Reckoning the material coincidences in St. Matthew to be 58 as above, the verbal coincidences would only amount to 16 or 17 ; in St. Mark the former would be 93 as compared with 17 of the latter; in St. Luke 41 as compared with 10. It further appears that by far the greater number of these verbal coincidences are met with in the report of our Lord's discourses and other sayings, a circumstance which confirms us in the belief that the Gospel was handed down for a number of years in an oral form, as the preachers and teachers would feel bound to adhere strictly to the very words in cases of reported speech, whereas they would be under no such obligation in the narration of events. As regards the latter, a considerable modification of the oral Gospel would naturally take place during the long period that elapsed before it was committed to writing. The modification would vary in different parts of the Church; and it is in this way, as well as by taking into account the possibility of fresh lessons being added from time to time by those who had been "eyewitnesses and ministers of the word" (Luke i. 2), that we can best account for differences, both in expression and in substance, which would otherwise seem unaccountable. If the apostles' teaching was originally given in Aramaic—the form of Hebrew then spoken in Palestine—and had to be translated into Greek by the catechists, this would help still further to account for the diversity we meet with in the Gospels.

5. Harmony.—It is possible that further study and investigation may shed more light on the historical and literary relations of the four Gospels, but meantime it is clear that the true way to discern their harmony is not to attempt to piece them together in the vain hope of forming a complete chronological history, but to study each from its own point of view and learn from it what it has to teach concerning the many-sided life and character of Jesus Christ. No one Gospel could possibly do justice to the infinite significance of the great theme; and instead of causing perplexity, the existence of four different

Gospels should rather be matter of thankfulness, as setting Christ before us in so many different aspects of His divinely human personality, much in the same way as various portions of the Old Testament set Him forth prophetically under the several aspects of prophet, priest, lawgiver, and king.

From the nature of the case, the Gospels are necessarily fragmentary, as indicated by St. John when he says "there are also many other things which Jesus did, the which, if they should be written every one, I suppose that even the world itself would not contain the books that should be written " (xxi. 25). The same writer gives us a key to the interpretation of his Gospel when he says, "These are written, that ye may believe that Jesus is the Christ, the Son of God; and that, believing, ye may have life in his name" (xx. 31). In like manner each of the other Gospels, while historical in its character, is animated by a special purpose of its own with its appropriate grouping and selection of events. Owing to the frequent change of scene and audience in Christ's ministry, the historical sequence could not be strictly adhered to by any one desirous to trace, from any point of view, the progress of His teaching. At the same time, there was a gradual development in His ministry, culminating in His death, resurrection, and ascension; and this gradual advance we find reflected in each of the four Gospels.

Unity amid diversity is what we have to look for in the Gospels, as in the Scriptures generally; and of this we have a token in the time-honoured fancy of the Church, by which the four Gospels are likened to the four-visaged cherubim, having the faces of a man, a lion, an ox, and an eagle. This comparison has been variously applied, but the interpretation followed in modern works of art, after St. Jerome, identifies the four faces with the Gospels of Matthew, Mark, Luke, and John respectively,

2

as setting forth the human, the conquering, the sacrificial, and the heaven-regarding aspects of Christ's being. We shall probably be nearer the truth, however, if we say that while the first Gospel sets forth Christ's life and teaching with reference to the *past*, as the fulfilment of the Old Testament, the Gospel of Mark exhibits that life in the *present* as a manifestation of the activity and power so congenial to the Roman mind; St. Luke, as a Greek, depicts it in its catholic and comprehensive character, as destined in the *future* to embrace within its saving influence all the kindreds of the Gentiles; while the fourth Gospel represents it in its absolute perfection as it is related to the Father in *eternity*.

While there is no such thing as uniformity in Scripture any more than in Nature or the Church, there is an essential and deep-lying unity which cannot be broken without serious injury to the truth. The right way to use the Gospels is to combine their various testimony, allowing each to tell its story in its own way and to contribute its allotted part to a full and adequate conception of the Lord's personality and work. While each possesses a distinct individuality of its own, they may and ought to be united in order to form a complete and grander whole. In this sense they have been likened to the four parts of music, which may be sung apart, but blend together to form a perfect harmony. A striking parallel has been drawn by Bishop Westcott[1] between the work of the first three evangelists and the threefold portrait of Charles I. (taken from three different points of view) which Vandyke prepared for the sculptor; while Dean Farrar[2] furnishes a beautiful illustration when he says that "the first three evangelists give us diverse aspects of one glorious landscape; St. John pours

[1] *Introduction to the Study of the Gospels*, p. 251.
[2] *Messages of the Books*, p. 11.

over that landscape a flood of heavenly sunshine which
seems to transform its very character, though every
feature of the landscape remains the same." [1]

[1] With regard to the harmony of the four Gospels in matters of
historical detail, while it is true that we meet with apparent discrepancies which it would require more complete information than we
possess to explain fully (for example, as to the date of the Last Supper,
whether on the night of the Jewish Passover, as the Synoptical Gospels
would lead us to suppose, or on the night previous, which is the
impression we receive from St. John's narrative), yet on the other hand
there are many cases of undesigned harmony which afford positive
evidence of their historical accuracy and truthfulness. (See Appendix
B, pp. 203, 204.)

CHAPTER III

1. Authorship.—St. Matthew's Gospel has been described by one who can scarcely be accused of partiality (M. Renan) as "the most important book of Christendom— the most important book that has ever been written." Its importance is derived, not from the genius of the writer, but from the grandeur of the subject. According to the unanimous tradition of the ancient Church, as preserved in the title which this Gospel has borne ever since the second century and confirmed by the testimony of the early Church Fathers beginning with Papias in the first half of the second century, the writer of the book was Matthew, one of the twelve apostles. But for his authorship of this book, Matthew would have been one of the least known of the apostles, as neither Scripture nor tradition gives us much information regarding him. Not a single word or act of his after he became a disciple of our Lord is recorded in the Gospels; and in the Book of Acts his name is never mentioned after the descent of the Holy Spirit on the day of Pentecost. He is evidently to be identified with Levi the publican (Mark ii. 14, 15; Luke v. 27-29; cf. Matt. ix. 9, 10), although it is only in his own Gospel (x. 3) that the despised term "publican" is associated

with his apostolic name of Matthew ("the gift of God"),
which was probably given to him when he was called to
the apostleship, as Simon's name was changed to Peter.
He seems to have been a man of worldly means and of a
generous disposition, judging from the fact that on the
occasion of his apostolic call, when "he forsook all, and
rose up and followed" Jesus, he made "a great feast" to
which he invited a number of his old associates. It is
noteworthy that he leaves it to the other evangelists to
mention him as the giver of this feast and to record his
sacrifice of property in following Christ; while we have a
further token of his modesty in the fact that he puts the
name of Thomas before his own in the list of apostles,
reversing the order followed in the other Gospels. Traces
of the writer's profession as a tax-gatherer have been
found in his use of the term "tribute money" (xxii. 19),
where the other evangelists employ the more common
word "penny" (Mark xii. 15; Luke xx. 24); and in his
use of the word "publicans" (v. 46, 47), where Luke
employs the word "sinners" (Luke vi. 32, 33). But
perhaps the latter instance, like his use of the word
"Gentiles" in the same passage, is an indication rather
of his Jewish nationality.

According to an ancient tradition derived from Papias,
Matthew wrote his Gospel in Hebrew, — to which
Irenæus adds that he published it among the Jews
"while Peter and Paul were preaching in Rome and
founding the Church there." Eusebius in the beginning
of the fourth century tells us that Matthew wrote it
when he was about to leave the Jews and preach also to
other nations, in order to "fill up the void about to be
made in his absence." If this tradition be correct, the
Hebrew original must have been very soon superseded by
the Greek Gospel which we now possess. This was only
to be expected, considering the growing disuse of Hebrew,

and the gradual lapse of the Jewish Christians into a heresy which alienated them from the rest of the Church.[1] Whether the Gospel was written over again by Matthew in Greek, or translated, perhaps under his supervision, by some other writer, with additions from a Greek source, is a question which we cannot certainly answer. That Matthew may have written the Gospel in both languages is in itself not unlikely, as we know that Josephus wrote his history both in Hebrew and in Greek—these two languages being both current in Palestine at that time, as English and Gaelic are now in the Highlands of Scotland.[2]

2. Date of Composition.—From evidence afforded by a study of the book itself (taken in connection with the tradition above mentioned), it has been reasonably inferred that the Gospel in its present form probably appeared before 66 A.D., when the war which was to issue in the destruction of the Jewish capital was on the eve of breaking out. Such evidence is found in the use of the expressions "holy city," "the holy place," "the city of the great King" (iv. 5; v. 35; xxiv. 15; xxvii. 53), as well as in the mysterious nature of the language used by the Saviour in His prediction of the city's coming doom. In particular, the caution given by the writer in xxiv. 15 ("whoso readeth, let him understand") would have had no force or meaning after the predicted calamity had occurred.

3. Character and Contents.—The leading charac-

---

[1] The *Ebionite* heresy, so named from a Hebrew word meaning *poor*, the early Jewish Christians being noted for their poverty. Their heresy consisted for the most part in holding the continued obligation of the Jewish Law, and denying the Divinity of the Saviour while admitting His Messiahship. The name of Nazarenes (originally given to Christians generally; Acts xxiv. 5) was applied in the fourth century to a less heretical sect who continued to observe the Jewish Law.

[2] Modern instances may also be found; *e.g.* Bacon published a Latin translation of his *Advancement of Learning*, in an extended form under the title *De Augmentis Scientiarum*. But it must be admitted to be a weak point in this theory that there is no trace of it in the writings of the Fathers.

teristic of St. Matthew's Gospel, as might be expected
in a work intended for the Hebrews, consists in the
representation of Jesus as *the Messiah*, in whom was
fulfilled the Law and the Prophets.   In this respect it is
fitly placed immediately after the Old Testament, as the
uniting link between the old and the new covenants.

The first verse strikes the keynote, "The book of the
generation of Jesus Christ, the son of David, the son of
Abraham"—son of David as the heir of the promised
kingdom, son of Abraham as the child of promise in
whom all the families of the earth were to be blessed.
The whole book may be regarded as depicting the
gradual realisation of these claims in a spiritual sense ;
the culminating point being reached in the glorious
declaration by the risen Lord, "All authority hath been
given unto me in heaven and on earth.   Go ye therefore
and make disciples of all the nations, baptizing them into
the name of the Father and of the Son and of the Holy
Ghost : teaching them to observe all things whatsoever I
commanded you : and lo, I am with you alway, even unto
the end of the world" (Matt. xxviii. 18-20).   In the
course of the Gospel there are no less than sixty citations
of Old Testament prophecy as fulfilled in Jesus, the usual
formula of quotation being "that it might be fulfilled
which was spoken by (the prophet)."   Equally significant
is the frequency of the expression "kingdom of heaven"
(literally "kingdom of the heavens," reflecting the
Hebrew idiom), which occurs thirty-two times, and the
designation "son of David," which occurs seven times as
applied to Jesus.

The whole plan of the book is in harmony with its
Messianic character.   First we have the nativity of Him
who was "born King of the Jews" and was at the same
time to "save his people from their sins" (chaps. i., ii.),
—with the strange mingling of light and shadow, of glory

and suffering, which was to be typical of the whole life. Then comes the Prelude to the Ministry (iii.-iv. 11), when the approach of the kingdom of heaven is announced by the predicted Forerunner; and the Baptism of Jesus, as the fulfilment of all righteousness and the consecration to His public ministry, becomes the signal for a manifesta-
tion of the divine favour in the voice from heaven, "This is my beloved Son, in whom I am well pleased,"—followed by the Temptation, in which the decisive choice is made between the "kingdoms of this world" and the unseen kingdom of the Spirit. The way is thus cleared for successive representations of the Saviour as Lawgiver, Prophet, and King. In the Sermon on the Mount (v.-vii.), the charter of the new kingdom, He proclaims the Law as from a second Sinai with new meaning and power,—a little later He charges the twelve apostles whom He commissions to preach the Gospel in His name (x.),—at another time He delivers the long series of parables in which the origin, progress, and final destiny of the kingdom are shown forth (xiii.),—anon He lays down the principles that are to guide the members of the Church in their relations to one another, especially to their erring brethren (xviii.) Then as the conflict with hatred and unbelief grows ever fiercer, there break forth His prophetic warnings of the nation's impending doom, and His denunciations against the Jewish priests and rulers, while He becomes more and more outspoken in the assertion of His Messianic claims (xxiii.-xxv.); till at last there comes the awful tragedy upon the Cross, com-
pleting the sacrifice He has to offer as God's High Priest, and giving place in turn to the triumph of the Resurrec-
tion (xxvi.-xxviii.) Interspersed throughout the whole are mighty works and gracious words, spoken and wrought for the suffering and the sinful, which bespeak Him as the Sent of God.

There is a wonderful symmetry in the whole narrative, and many subtle contrasts. In xvi. 21, "From that time began Jesus to shew unto his disciples how that he must go unto Jerusalem and suffer . . . and be killed," there is a striking contrast to iv. 17, "From that time began Jesus to preach, and to say, Repent ye: for the kingdom of heaven is at hand"—the one marking the commencement of His Passion, as the other of His active Ministry. There is a correspondence also between the voice from heaven at His Baptism (iii. 17), and that heard at His Transfiguration (xvii. 5), when His ministry reached its climax and was sealed by the divine testimony in the presence of the two greatest prophets of the old covenant, Moses and Elias, as it had just before been attested by the great confession of Peter (xvi. 16). That confession was a token that the ministry of power and love had done its work upon the hearts of the disciples, and it is fitly followed by the announcement of His appointed sufferings, the disciples being now ready to follow their Master through the valley of His humiliation, which was to conduct them at last from the blackness and darkness of death to the glories of divine life and immortality.

A distinguishing feature of this Gospel is the large place assigned in it to the *words* [1] of Jesus, arranged in a *systematic* form, not broken up into fragments as they are in the other Gospels. For this reason Godet compares Luke to "a botanist who prefers to contemplate a flower in the very place of its birth and in the midst of its natural surroundings, while Matthew is like the gardener who for some special object puts together large and magnificent bouquets." To some extent this remark is applicable to Matthew's grouping of incidents in our Lord's life, as well as to his arrangement of discourses.

[1] Forming about a fourth part of the whole book.

CHAPTER IV

1. Authorship.—The testimony of the early Fathers, so far as it has reached us, unanimously ascribes the second Gospel to St. Mark; but with equal unanimity they connect it with the preaching of the Apostle Peter. The earliest witness is Papias, the bishop already referred to, who makes the following statement on the authority of John, a contemporary of the apostles if not the apostle of that name. "This also the elder used to say: Mark having become Peter's interpreter, wrote accurately all that he remembered of the things that were either said or done by Christ; but not in order. For he neither heard the Lord nor followed Him; but subsequently, as I said, attached himself to Peter, who used to frame his teaching to meet the wants of his hearers, but not as making a connected narrative of our Lord's oracles (or discourses). So Mark committed no error in thus writing down particulars just as he remembered them; for he took heed to one thing, to omit none of the things that he had heard, and to state nothing falsely in his account of them."

So little doubt seems to have been entertained regarding the Petrine authorship of this Gospel that we find Justin Martyr apparently referring to it as the

Memoirs of Peter. According to Irenæus, it was written by Mark at Rome after the death of Peter and Paul; while Clement of Alexandria, writing about the same time, affirms, on the tradition of a long line of presbyters, that St. Mark wrote at the request of Peter's hearers at Rome, without any interference on the part of Peter himself.

Regarding the history of the Mark thus referred to, and his relations with the Apostle Peter, we derive information from Scripture which is fitted to corroborate in a great measure the ancient tradition. There can be no doubt that we are to identify him with the John Mark mentioned in Acts xii. 12, whose mother Mary was an influential member of the Church at Jerusalem—her house being the place where prayer was made for Peter by the brethren during his imprisonment, and where he himself repaired immediately after his liberation. It is an interesting conjecture that this house may have been the scene of the Last Supper and of the Pentecostal effusion of the Holy Spirit. It has also been suggested that the "young man" referred to in Mark's Gospel, in connection with the arrest in the garden, may have been none other than the author of the book, who was thus led to record an incident which to others would have appeared insignificant (xiv. 51). Mark's intimacy with Peter at a later time is evident from 1 Peter v. 13, where the apostle conveys Mark's salutation to his readers in Asia Minor; and from the designation which Peter there applies to him ("my son"), we may infer that he was one of that apostle's converts. It appears that at the time the epistle was written he was residing with Peter in Babylon, but although the Eastern city of that name was then, and continued to be for long afterwards, a famous seat of Jewish learning, there is reason to believe that in the passage referred to Babylon is only another

name for Rome (p. 167). Previous to his association
with Peter in apostolic work abroad, Mark had accompanied Paul and Barnabas as their "minister" or
assistant, but had withdrawn from the work (Acts xiii. 5,
13). After an interval of some years, he rejoined his
cousin Barnabas, whose willingness to receive him again
as a colleague was so displeasing to Paul that he parted
company with Barnabas on this account (Acts. xv. 37-39).
We find him again enjoying Paul's confidence, however,
during the imprisonment of the latter at Rome ; for the
apostle commends him to the Colossians as one of his
"fellow-workers unto the kingdom of God," who had been
a "comfort" to him (Col. iv. 10, 11 ; Philemon, ver. 24).
Mark was then, apparently, about to set out for Asia ;
and, accordingly, we find Paul, during his second imprisonment, requesting Timothy to bring him with him (from
Ephesus), because he was "useful to him for ministering"
(2 Tim. iv. 11). This is the last time we hear of Mark
in Scripture ; but according to tradition he returned to
Rome, and after the martyrdom of Peter and Paul, went
to Alexandria, where he founded a famous catechetical
school, and died a martyr's death.[1]

Turning now to internal evidence, we find strong confirmation of the traditional account. The book may be
described as very much an expansion or development
of the brief statement made by Peter in his address to
Cornelius and his friends (Acts x. 36-42). It also follows
closely the line of apostolic testimony which Peter had
himself marked out immediately after the Ascension
(Acts i. 22). The whole tone of the book reflects Peter's
energetic, impulsive, unconventional character. Its *rapid
transition* from one incident to another, of which we

---

[1] In the ninth century St. Mark's body is said to have been trans-
ported from Alexandria to Venice, where he has been honoured as
patron-saint ever since.

have a striking illustration in the fact that the Greek
word variously translated "straightway," "immediately,"
"forthwith," etc., occurs in it no less than forty-one times;[1]
its *practical matter-of-fact tone*, illustrated by the circumstance that it records eighteen miracles but only four
parables,[2] while it twice represents the Lord and His
disciples as having their hands so full of work that
"they could not so much as eat bread" (iii. 20; vi. 31);
its *vivid description of the excitement* occasioned by Christ's
ministry, and of the profound impression made on those who
heard and saw Him, which would be a subject congenial
to Peter's enthusiastic nature (i. 27; ii. 2, 12; vi. 33,
etc.); its *omission* of some things redounding to Peter's
credit, *e.g.* his designation as the rock on which the
Church was to be built (viii. 29, 30; cf. Matt. xvi. 16-19),
and the *insertion* of other things fitted to humble him,
such as the rebuke he received when he would have
dissuaded Jesus from submitting to His appointed sufferings (viii. 33), and the warning he received by the first
crowing of the cock (xiv. 30, 68-72), as well as the
introduction of details which would be likely to dwell in
Peter's memory (i. 36; xi. 21; xvi. 7)—all these things
lend a high degree of probability to the traditional
account of Peter's connection with this Gospel. As
regards that part of the tradition which represents the
Gospel as having been written at Rome for the Christians
there, we find confirmation of it in the *connection of
Mark with Rome* already referred to, and in his *Roman
name "Marcus,"* which gradually superseded the Hebrew
"John"; in the *absence of the Hebrew genealogy* of our

---

[1] Only eighteen times in Matthew, and eight times in Luke.

[2] Viz. the Sower, the Mustard seed, the wicked Husbandman, and
the Seed growing secretly,—the last being peculiar to this Gospel. It
is "the kingdom of God" they refer to—an expression that is characteristic of Mark and Luke, as distinguished from "the kingdom of
heaven," which is the usual form in Matthew's Gospel.

Lord ; in the *explanation of Jewish words, e.g.* Boanerges
("which is Sons of Thunder"), Talitha cumi ("which
is being interpreted, Damsel, I say unto thee, Arise"),
Corban ("that is to say, Given"), Ephphatha ("that
is, Be opened"), Abba ("Father") (iii. 17; v. 41; vii. 11;
vii. 34; xiv. 36);[1] and of *Jewish customs, e.g.* the washing
of hands (vii. 3, 4), and Passover observances (xiv. 12;
xv. 42); in the frequent use of *Latin words and idioms,
e.g.* "legion," "centurion," "quadrantes"—the Roman
equivalent to two Jewish mites (xii. 42); and very
specially in the mention of *Alexander and Rufus* (xv. 21),
if the latter be, as seems very probable, the same person
as is referred to by St. Paul in his Epistle to the Romans
—xvi. 13.

2. Date of Composition.—With regard to the date of
the Gospel we may conclude in the light of what has
been already mentioned that it was written between
64 A.D. and 68 A.D.—the latter being the year of Nero's
death, in whose reign Peter and Paul are believed to have
suffered martyrdom.[2]

3. Character and Contents.—If the first Gospel may
be described as Messianic, the second may be fitly styled
realistic, bearing traces throughout of the graphic report
of an eyewitness.

It is *minute and circumstantial*, giving many details
of person, number, place, and time that are not to be
found in the other Gospels (xiii. 3; vi. 7; xii. 41; i. 35).

---

[1] The preservation of these Aramaic expressions is a token of fidelity
to the original tradition.

[2] It contains, like the first Gospel, a prophecy of the Destruction
of Jerusalem, in a form which implies that the great event had not
yet taken place. See especially the parenthetic expression in xiii. 14
("let him that readeth understand"). If we accept the suggestion
above mentioned, that it is the same Rufus that is named in xv. 21
and in Rom. xvi. 13, this also is so far a confirmation of its apostolic
date. The "rudeness" of its Greek and its comparative inattention
to doctrinal interests are acknowledged signs of its primitive character.

It gives a *vivid description* of the emotions, looks, gestures, and actions of our Lord and others (iii. 5, 34 ; vii. 33 ; viii. 33 ; ix. 36 ; x. 32, etc.) It brings out the *picturesque character* of many of the scenes enacted in our Lord's ministry, *e.g.* in the narrative of the feeding of the five thousand (vi. 35-44) this Gospel "alone tells us of the fresh green grass on which they sat down by hundreds and by fifties ; and the word used for 'companies' means literally 'flower - beds,' as though to St. Peter those multitudes, in their festal passover attire with its many-coloured Oriental brightness of red and blue, looked like the patches of crocus and poppy and tulip and amaryllis which he had seen upon the mountain slopes." In keeping with this is the *photographic character* of its account of the Transfiguration[1] and the cure of the demoniac boy (ix.), and of the Storm on the Sea of Gennesaret (iv. 35-41). It also frequently reproduces *the very words* of Jesus (iv. 39 ; vi. 31 ; cf. Matt. viii. 26) and of others (vi. 22-25), using the term "Rabbi," or teacher ("Master"), as the earlier mode of addressing Jesus, where the other evangelists prefer "Lord"[2] (iv. 38 ; ix. 5 ; x. 51 ; cf. Matt. viii. 25 ; xvii. 4 ; xx. 30-33), and narrates events in the *present tense* as if they were just taking place (i. 40 ; xiv. 43).

Altogether, it is a simple, direct, forcible narrative, and gives the general outline of our Lord's ministry in a clearer form than either the Gospel of Matthew or Luke. It sets Him before us as He worked and taught in the living present, making no mention of the law, and scarcely ever quoting prophecy, but aiming simply to depict Him in that aspect of energetic and victorious

---

[1] Raffaelle is mainly indebted to this Gospel for the details of his great picture.

[2] We find a similar instance of *literal accuracy* in the habitual use of the name "Simon" in the beginning of the Gospel, before the apostolic name of Peter had been conferred (i. 16, 29, 30, 36).

strength which was fitted to impress the Roman mind,
and which is foreshadowed by the opening words, "The
beginning of the gospel of Jesus Christ the Son of God."

The following are the passages peculiar to Mark's
Gospel :—

> The alarm of Jesus' family (iii. 21).
> The seed growing secretly (iv. 26-29).
> The healing of one deaf and dumb (vii. 32-37).
> The gradual healing of the blind man (viii. 22-26).
> The exhortation to watch (xiii. 33-37).
> The flight of the young man (xiv. 51, 52).
> Certain details about the Lord's Resurrection
> (xvi. 6-11).

In this connection it may be well to recall the fact
that while Mark's Gospel has a larger proportion of
common matter than any of the others—amounting to
no less than 93 per cent of its whole contents—this
is probably due, not to its having borrowed from the
others, but to its more strict adherence to the original
cycle of oral teaching (pp. 10-13).

Note.—Verses 9-20 in the last chapter are absent from
some ancient MSS. (see marginal note, R.V.) The verses
referred to differ greatly in style and language from the
rest of the book, and on this account it has been supposed
that they were added by a later hand (possibly with the
aid of an independent record), not long after the publication of the Gospel, in order to give a suitable close to
the narrative.

CHAPTER V

"THE GOSPEL ACCORDING TO ST. LUKE"

1. Authorship.—The authorship of the third Gospel has scarcely ever been disputed. It has uniformly been ascribed to Luke, the friend and companion of the Apostle Paul.

A comparison of its opening verses with the preface to the Book of Acts, and an examination of the style and structure of the two books, leave no room for doubt that they were written by one and the same person. The indications of his personality afforded by certain passages in the Book of Acts, where he joins himself with Paul by the use of the first person plural as if he were in his company at the time—viewed in the light of the information afforded by the Book of Acts and the epistles of Paul, regarding the apostle's personal associates and his relations with them,—justify us in holding that the early Church was right in ascribing the authorship to Luke.[1]

[1] An examination of the relative passages, which are too numerous to mention, shows that there are only three of the apostle's friends who could have been with him on the occasions referred to, viz. Luke, Jesus Justus, and Demas. But Demas is disqualified by 2 Tim. iv. 10 ("for Demas forsook me, having loved this present world"), while Jesus Justus is referred to as "of the circumcision" (Col. iv. 11), whereas the tone, both of the third Gospel and of the Book of Acts, would lead us to suppose that the author was a Gentile. The details are given in Birks' *Horæ Apostolicæ*, p. 351.

3

With regard to Luke's personal history, nearly all that we know of him is connected with the apostolic labours of Paul. He is referred to by that apostle as "the beloved physician" (Cól. iv. 14), and it has been suggested that it may have been owing to Paul's need of medical attendance that they were first brought into intimate relations with one another (Acts xvi. 6-10; Gal. iv. 13-15). Traces of Luke's profession have been discovered in the frequency with which he refers to Christ's work and that of His apostles as a ministry of *healing* (iv. 18, 23; ix. 1, 2, 6; x. 9; cf. also xxii. 51, which tells of the healing of Malchus' ear, a fact unrecorded by any of the other three evangelists in their account of the incident), as well as in the occasional use of *technical* and other forms of expression which a physician was likely to employ (iv. 38; v. 12; vi. 19; xxii. 44).[1]

It has been supposed, not without reason, that it is Luke who is referred to (2 Cor. viii. 18) as "the brother whose praise in the gospel is spread through all the churches";[2] but whether this be so or not, we have incontestable evidence that Luke was not only a warm friend of the apostle but a valuable coadjutor. In the Epistle to Philemon (ver. 24), which was written during

---

[1] With regard to the tradition that Luke was a painter, expressed in Rossetti's lines

> " Give honour unto Luke, evangelist,
>   For he it was, the ancient legends say,
>   Who first taught Art to fold her hands and pray,'

there is no authority of any value to support it, although not a few old pictures in Italy are shown to the credulous as the work of Luke. But, though "not written by a painter, this is yet a painter's Gospel. From it come the favourite subjects :—the Virgin and Child, Simeon, the Scene with the Doctors in the Temple, the Ascension " (Alexander's *Leading Ideas of the Gospels*).

[2] We have an ancient memorial of this belief in the superscription at the close of the epistle. "The gospel" is here to be taken in a general sense, not as referring to the Gospel by Luke.

Paul's first imprisonment in Rome, Luke is one of Paul's "fellow-workers" who send greetings, and in 2 Timothy (iv. 11), which was written during Paul's second imprisonment when many of his friends had forsaken him, we find the brief but weighty statement, "Only Luke is with me."

Of Luke's nationality and of his history previous to his association with the apostle we have but scanty information. From the distinction drawn between him and those "of the circumcision" (Col. iv. 11-14) it may be inferred that he was of Gentile extraction; and this inference is confirmed by his Greek name and the character of his style, which—except when he is drawing from older documents or reporting speeches conveyed to him by others—is more classical than that of the other Gospels, in the structure of the sentences and the choice of words, as well as in the use of an opening dedication, which is a feature quite foreign to the Hebrew style. According to Eusebius and Jerome, who wrote in the fourth century, Luke was a native of Antioch in Syria. Of this confirmation is found in the full account he gives of the Church at Antioch, and also in his description of Nicolas as "a proselyte *of Antioch*" (Acts vi. 5).[1] But the place where Luke seems to have been most at home and to have rendered the greatest service was Philippi, and with that city some modern writers connect him. His meeting with Paul at Troas (Acts xvi. 10) seems to have had a close bearing on the apostle's mission to Europe; and if he was a native of Philippi, this would account for their going to preach there first, and for Luke's rejoining

---

[1] A parallel has been drawn between this circumstance and the mention made by two *Scottish* authors alone (Scott and Alison), out of eight writers who give an account of Napoleon's Russian campaign, of the fact that General Barclay de Tolly was of *Scottish* extraction.

the apostle in the same city six or seven years afterwards (see p. 51, note 1).[1]

While tradition has always ascribed the third Gospel to Luke, it has assigned to Paul a somewhat similar part in its production to that which Peter bore in relation to the Gospel of Mark.   Such a connection is rendered probable both by what we know of the relations between Paul and Luke, and by the character of the Gospel itself, which is so liberal and philanthropic in its tone as to form an excellent *historic groundwork for the doctrine of salvation by grace through faith*, which was characteristic of Paul's preaching.[2]   There is also a striking similarity between the words attributed to our Lord in *the institution of the Supper* (xxii. 19, 20) and those in 1 Cor. xi. 24, 25 (Luke having doubtless often heard Paul use the words in the celebration of the Sacrament), as well as in the accounts which the two books give of our *Lord's appearances after His Resurrection* (Luke xxiv. ; 1 Cor. xv. 1-7).   The duty of *prayer* and the influence of the *Holy Spirit*, which figure so largely in this Gospel,[3] are also characteristic of Paul's writings ; and there are certain forms of expression which are common to them both, *e.g. a threefold classification of ideas* (xv. 3, 8, 11 ; ix. 57-62 ; xi. 11, 12 ; cf. 1 Cor. xiii. 13 ; Eph. iv. 4-6).

[1] In *The Expositor*, May 1895, p. 395, Professor Ramsay says : "That Renan was right about Luke's European and Macedonian origin I cannot doubt.   *Acts* is the composition of a Greek, and specially of a Macedonian ; its peculiar tone and emotion can be explained or appreciated on no other view."

[2] This is the element of truth lying at the bottom of the Tübingen theory, which represents the third Gospel as an attempt to magnify Paul at the expense of the Judaizers.

[3] It represents Jesus praying—at His baptism (iii. 21) ; before choosing His apostles (vi. 12, 13) ; at His transfiguration (ix. 28, 29) ; for His murderers (xxiii. 34) ; and commending His spirit into His Father's hands (xxiii. 46).   It has two parables inculcating earnestness in prayer : the appeal to friend at midnight (xi. 5-13) ; the importunate widow (xviii. 1-8).   The Holy Spirit is mentioned four times in the first chapter, viz. at verses 15, 35, 41, 67.

From his preface we learn that it was Luke's object to draw up in as complete and consecutive a form as possible an account of the main facts regarding Christ's person and work, by reference to the most authentic and reliable sources of information. His missionary travels with Paul would afford excellent opportunities for collecting such information. In particular the two years which he seems to have spent in Cæsarea during Paul's detention by Felix, where he was within two days' journey of the shores of Lake Gennesaret, the scene of many incidents in our Lord's ministry, would enable him to obtain at first hand, from brethren who had been eyewitnesses, many of those narratives which are only to be found in this Gospel.[1] His high Christian character gave him a moral fitness for the work, while his culture and the love of accuracy manifest in his historical and topographical allusions,[2] marked him out as a suitable instrument in the hands of Providence for writing the Gospel story in a form as well adapted for the philosophical Greeks as Matthew's Gospel was to be for the theocratic Jews and Mark's for the practical Romans.

2. Date of Composition.—The date of its composition is uncertain. It may have been as early as 60 A.D., at the close of the two years which Luke spent with Paul at Cæsarea ; or it may possibly have been during Paul's im-

---

[1] No doubt sometimes delivered orally and sometimes in the form of a written narrative, as indicated in i. 1. Hence the contrast between the Aramaic style of the Gospel generally (and of the earlier part of the Book of Acts) and the classical Greek of Luke's own opening dedication. His informant with regard to the Saviour's infancy and childhood may have been no other than Mary herself.

[2] *E.g.* in giving dates (ii. 2, iii. 1-3) and in the mention of our Saviour's age when He began His public ministry (iii. 23). But see p. 54 (on the Book of Acts) : " The man who in the anxiety and weariness of a tempestuous voyage, even in a wreck, was able to observe and record with such demonstrated accuracy the incidents of his adventure, must be worthy of credit in any case in which he pledges himself to have carefully investigated the facts that he records as true."

prisonment at Rome, 61-63 A.D., or even some years later; but in any case anterior to the Book of Acts, as the preface to the latter implies.

3. Character and Contents.—If St. Matthew's Gospel may be styled the *Messianic* Gospel and St. Mark's the *realistic* Gospel, St. Luke's may be fitly described as the *catholic* Gospel — foreshadowing the expansion of God's kingdom in the future as the first Gospel reflects its history in the past, and the second describes its energy in the present. It is not only more comprehensive in its range, beginning with the birth of the forerunner and ending with an account of the Ascension,[1] but it also brings out more fully the breadth of Christ's sympathy and the fulness and freeness of His love. In illustration of this we may note the following points: (1) The Gospel of Luke traces Christ's genealogy, not, as Matthew's does, by the legal line to Abraham, the head of the Jews, but by the *natural line to Adam,* the head of humanity (iii. 38), forming thus a fit introduction to the life of Him who was to be the Kinsman - Redeemer of the whole human family. (2) It exhibits more clearly the reality of Christ's *humanity* in the various stages of human life (ii. 4-7, ii. 21, 22, ii. 40, ii. 42, ii. 51, 52, iii. 23), and brings into special prominence His dependence upon God in the great crises of His life, when He had recourse to Him in *prayer* (iii. 21; vi. 12, 13; ix. 28, 29; xxiii. 34, 46), while it inculcates earnestness in prayer by two parables peculiar to itself (xi. 5-13; xviii. 1-8). (3) In keeping with this view of it as the gospel of humanity, we find that it represents Christ's *teaching* not so much in its theocratic as in its *human aspects*—its usual formula

---

[1] No information is given with regard to either of these events in any of the other Gospels, except the bare allusion to the Ascension in the disputed passage of Mark (xvi. 19): "So then the Lord Jesus, after he had spoken unto them, was received up into heaven, and sat down at the right hand of God."

in the introduction of a parable being not "the kingdom
of heaven is like," as in Matthew's, but "a certain man
made a great supper" (xiv. 16), "a certain man had two
sons" (xv. 11), etc. (4) It represents Christ as *far-
reaching in His sympathies*, full of compassion for the
poor, the weak, the suffering, and ready to forgive the
chief of sinners. It is in this Gospel we find the parables
of The Rich Man and Lazarus (xvi. 19), The Pharisee
and Publican (xviii. 9), The Prodigal Son (xv. 11), and
The Two Debtors (vii. 41-43). It is here we find a record
of Christ's visit to the house of Zacchæus the publican
(xix. 1), of His gracious reception of the woman that was
a sinner (vii. 37), of His prayer for His murderers (xxiii.
34), and of His promise of Paradise to the penitent
malefactor (xxiii. 43). It is here we find the touching
story of the raising to life of the young man at the gate
of Nain (vii. 11), who was "the only son of his mother,
and she was a widow"; it is here we are told that Jairus'
daughter, whom Christ restored to life, was an "only
daughter" (viii. 42); it is here we learn that the demoniac boy whom He healed at the foot of the Mount of
Transfiguration was an "only child" (ix. 38). (5) It is the
Gospel of *toleration and large-heartedness*, embracing within
the range of its sympathy the *Samaritan* (ix. 51-56; x.
25-37; xvii. 11-19), the *Gentile* (iv. 25-27; xiii. 28, 29), the
poor (ii. 7, 8, 24; vi. 20; ix. 58; xiv. 21), the *very young* (this
being the only Gospel that tells us that the children brought
to Jesus were "babes," xviii. 15, R.V.), and the *weaker* and,
up to that time, *less-honoured sex* (i. concerning Mary and
Elisabeth; ii. 36-38; viii. 1-3; x. 38-42; xxiii. 27, 28).

It is no accident, therefore, that the words "Saviour,"
"salvation," "grace," occur more frequently in this than
in any other Gospel; [1] it is no accident that it represents

---

[1] They are to be found in the fourth Gospel, but not at all in
Matthew or Mark.

the Saviour's birth as heralded by angels[1] to shepherds watching their flocks by night (ii. 8-14), and His ministry as opening in a despised village of Galilee with the gracious words of the evangelic prophet, "The spirit of the Lord is upon me, because he anointed me to preach good tidings to the poor" (iv. 18); it is no accident that as its first chapters resound with the voice of praise and thanksgiving for the birth of the Saviour, its closing verses tell of the disciples' joy as they returned to Jerusalem with the blessing of the Ascended Saviour resting on their heads, to be "continually in the temple, blessing God." It is because this Gospel from first to last tells the "good tidings of great joy which shall be to all the people" (ii. 10), and proclaims a Saviour who is to be "a light for revelation to the Gentiles and the glory of (Thy people) Israel" (ii. 32),—in whose name "repentance and remission of sins should be preached unto all the nations, beginning from Jerusalem" (xxiv. 47). Luke is indeed the most evangelical of all the evangelists, and as such he has fitly preserved for us the first precious germs of Christian hymnology, which, after eighteen centuries, are still prized as an aid to worship by almost all sections of the Christian Church, viz. the Magnificat (i. 46-55), the Benedictus (i. 68-79), the Gloria in Excelsis (ii. 14), and the Nunc Dimittis (ii. 29-32).

It adds to the importance of this Gospel, styled by Renan "the most beautiful book in the world," that about one-third of its contents is peculiar to itself, consisting mainly of chapters ix. 51–xviii. 14, relating to the Saviour's last journey to Jerusalem.

---

[1] ii. 8-14. The ministry of angels both to Christ and to His people is more prominent in this than in any other Gospel; the same feature is noticeable in the Book of Acts, in which angels are mentioned twenty-two times.

CHAPTER VI

1. Authorship.—It is a weighty and significant fact that until the close of the last century the Johannine authorship of the fourth Gospel was never seriously challenged. Epiphanius, indeed (380 A.D.), tells us of a very small party who had ascribed it to Cerinthus, a heretical contemporary of the Apostle John at Ephesus; but they seem to have had no other reason for rejecting it than their aversion to its teaching. During the present century no question has been the subject of more controversy; and scarcely any can be of more importance, considering its close bearing on the doctrinal aspects of Christianity, and especially on the divinity of Jesus Christ.

To a large extent the question is overtaken by the line of evidence already indicated in connection with the Gospels as a whole (Chap. II. § 2). Although not quoted by name till late in the second century (by Theophilus), the external evidence for this Gospel is in some respects stronger than for any of the others. It is specially quoted by such early Gnostic writers as Basilides (125 A.D.), Valentinus (145 A.D., whose favourite phrases were borrowed from its opening verses), and Heracleon (a disciple of Valentinus), who wrote a commentary on it —being the first known commentary on any part of the

New Testament.   It has also to be borne in mind that
John himself survived till near the close of the first
century, so that a comparatively short interval was left
between his death and the time when the four Gospels
are known to have been universally accepted by the
Church (185 A.D.).   For this interval it so happens that,
apart from the Gnostic testimony already adduced, we
have a direct chain of testimony consisting of a very few
strong and well-connected links.   At the lower end of
the chain we have Irenæus, one of the most important
witnesses to the general reception of the four Gospels
towards the close of the second century.   Born in Asia
Minor, where John spent the last twenty or thirty years
of his life, he became Bishop of Lyons in Gaul, which
had a close ecclesiastical connection with his native land.
Early in life he was brought into familiar contact with
Polycarp (born 70 A.D.), a disciple of the Apostle John,
who was for more than forty years Bishop of Smyrna and
was martyred 155-156 A.D.   Among other allusions which
Irenæus makes to Polycarp, he says, in a letter to his
friend Florinus (177 A.D.), " I can describe the very place
in which the blessed Polycarp used to sit when he dis-
coursed, and his goings out and his comings in, and his
manner of life and his personal appearance, and the discourses which he held before the people, and how he
would describe his intercourse with John and with the
rest who had seen the Lord, and how he would relate their
words.   And whatsoever things he had heard from them
about the Lord and about His miracles, Polycarp, as
having received them from eye-witnesses of the life of
the Word, would relate altogether in accordance with the
Scriptures."
    It is beyond dispute that this Irenæus had accepted
the fourth Gospel as a genuine work of the Apostle John.
Is it credible that he would have done so, if it had not

been acknowledged by his teacher Polycarp, who had been a disciple of John? And if it was accepted by Polycarp as a genuine writing, notwithstanding its marked dissimilarity to the other Gospels, what better evidence could we have that John was really its author, and that it was accepted as his, from the very first, by the leaders of the Church in Asia Minor?[1]

The following are the principal facts in John's life, and the circumstances under which he is said to have written his Gospel.

The younger son of Zebedee, a Galilean fisherman, who was in a position to have " hired servants," he was a follower of the Baptist before joining Christ's fellowship. To his mother Salome (supposed by some to be the sister of the Virgin Mary, Mark xv. 40 ; John xix. 25), who was one of the most devoted followers of Jesus, he and his brother James seem to have been indebted for much of their enthusiasm. They were surnamed by Jesus "Boanerges" (sons of thunder), in allusion to the latent fervour and vehemence of their nature, of which we are not without tokens (Matt. xx. 20-24 ; Luke ix. 49-54). During Christ's trial and crucifixion John was a close and deeply-interested observer, receiving a charge from his dying Master to act the part of a son to the bereaved Mary, which he faithfully carried out (John xviii. 15, 16 ; xix. 25, 26). After the resurrection we find him associated with Peter on several important occasions (Acts iii., iv.), but not a single discourse of his is recorded in the Book of Acts. He still continued, however, to be revered as a leader of the Church, for we find him referred to by St. Paul (Gal. ii. 9), apparently in

---

[1] This argument is further strengthened by the fact that not a few quotations from this Gospel are found in the writings of Justin Martyr, who wrote before the middle of the second century, and was well acquainted with the teaching of the Church in Asia Minor, his Dialogue with Trypho the Jew having taken place in Ephesus.

connection with the Council of Jerusalem (50 A.D.), as one of those who were "reputed to be pillars." In his later life, after the fall of Jerusalem (70 A.D.), according to a general and well-supported tradition, John resided in Ephesus, as bishop of the Churches in Asia Minor which had been founded by Paul, and was banished under Domitian to the island of Patmos (where he wrote the Book of Revelation, Rev. i. 9), returning to Ephesus in the reign of Nerva, and living there till after the accession of Trajan (98 A.D.).

It was in Ephesus, which had now become the chief centre of Christianity, and was beginning to be infected by the errors of which Paul had warned its elders at Miletus (Acts xx. 29, 30), that the earliest traditions represent John to have written his Gospel. He is said to have done so on the entreaty, and with the subsequent approval, of the Apostle Andrew and other leading members of the Church, in order to supplement the teaching of the three Gospels already published, and to counteract the errors which were beguiling some from the simplicity of the faith.

Turning now to the evidence of its authorship afforded by the Gospel itself, we may first of all note the fact that the whole tone of the book would give one the impression that it was written by some one who was *familiar with the inner life of Christ and His apostles* (i. 35-51 ; ii. 11, 17, 22 ; iv. 6, 8, 27 ; vi. 5, 8, 68-71 ; ix. 2 ; xi. 16 ; xii. 21, 22 ; xiii. ; xviii. 16 ; xx.). This circumstance points to one of the twelve disciples as the author—in accordance with the statement (i. 14), " We beheld his glory, glory as of the only begotten from the Father," and the explicit declaration in the 24th verse of the last chapter (the whole of which seems to form a postscript added by the apostle and endorsed by his companions),—" This is the disciple which beareth wit-

ness of these things, and wrote these things : and we
know that his witness is true." As to which of the
disciples is here meant, we find a clue in verse 20 of the
same chapter, which identifies him with "the disciple
whom Jesus loved," who had been previously referred to
in xx. 2, and xxi. 7, in association with Peter, and in
xiii. 23, where he is described as "reclining in Jesus'
bosom" at the Last Supper. The presumption that the
disciple thus designated was one of the sons of Zebedee,
who were admitted along with Peter (as the other evangelists tell us) to a closer fellowship with their Master
than the rest of the disciples, is strengthened by the
remarkable circumstance that the two brothers are never
mentioned in this Gospel, except in the second verse
of the last chapter where they are referred to as
"the sons of Zebedee." The position there assigned
to them in the list of disciples is much lower than is
usual in the other Gospels, and confirms us in the supposition that it was modesty that led the author to veil
his own name (i. 35-42; xviii. 15, 16; xix. 26, 27), as
well as that of his brother James and his mother Salome
(whom he nowhere mentions unless at xix. 25), as he is
in general very precise and explicit in his mode of designation. As between the two brothers, there can be no
hesitation in assigning the authorship to John, since
James early fell a victim to the Herodian persecution
44 A.D. (Acts xii. 2).

If the Gospel was not written by John, it must have
been written by some one who wished to pass for that
apostle. But where shall we find a writer of the post-
apostolic age possessed of the intellectual gifts and the
spiritual elevation needed for the production of so sublime
a work, a writer, at the same time, unscrupulous enough
to claim for his fabrications, in the most solemn terms,
the authority of an eye-witness and apostle who had

reclined in Jesus' bosom? For those who reject the Johannine authorship this amounts to an insuperable difficulty.[1]

Besides the allusions to the inner life of Christ and His apostles which have already been referred to, there may be discerned in this Gospel, on a close examination, many other tokens of its apostolic origin.

(1) In its account of Christ's ministry it gives a faithful picture of the *Messianic expectations* which existed among the Jews prior to the destruction of Jerusalem, as well as of the conflict which Christ waged with their hopes of temporal sovereignty (i. 19-28 ; iv. 25 ; vi. 14, 15 ; vii. ; xi. 47-53 ; xix. 12) ; while we also find traces of acquaintance with the *Temple arrangements* of the same period (ii. 13-16 ; iv. 20, 21 ; x. 23).

(2) It shows a minute acquaintance with *Jewish customs* (ii. 6 ; iii. 25 ; vii. 22 ; xi. 55 ; xix. 7, 31), *manners* (iv. 9, 27 ; vii. 2, 37 ; x. 22 ; xi. 44 ; xviii. 28 ; xix. 40), and *opinions* (i. 46 ; vii. 35, 41, 52 ; ix. 2, 16 ; x. 19-21), frequently giving *explanations* as if it were written by a Jew for foreign readers.

(3) It also shows a minute acquaintance with the *topography* of Jerusalem (v. 2 ; viii. 20 ; ix. 7 ; xi. 18 ; xviii. 1, 15 ; xix. 13, 17, 41), and with the *geography* of Palestine generally (i. 28 ; iii. 23 ; iv. 5, 35 ; xi. 54).

(4) It is *circumstantial in many of its statements*, and graphic in its delineation of character, bearing the stamp

---

[1] From the writings of the Apostles to those of the Apostolic Fathers is a great descent. "Speaking broadly, we may say, from the intellectual point of view, the men (of the sub-Apostolic age) have hardly begun to understand the alphabet of the religion" (Dr. A. M. Fairbairn). "We have to go to the fourth century, to the time of Chrysostom and Augustine, before we find any Christian writer whom it would not be absurd to regard as capable, even with the help of the Synoptic Gospels, of putting together such discourses as those in the Fourth Gospel" (Peabody). The character of the Apocryphal Gospels, in particular, confirms this view.

of personal knowledge such as would be possessed by an *eye-witness* (i. 29, 35-43 ; ii. 1, 20 ; iv. 6, 40, 52 ; vi. 16-24, x. 40, xi. 6, 39, etc.; xii. 1, xviii. 10, etc.; xix., 25, xx. 1-10, etc.).[1]

(5) While written in Greek, it is *Hebraic in its style and structure*, abounding in parallels and contrasts, both in expression and arrangement, and being marked by great simplicity of syntax (*e.g.* chap. i.), and it frequently quotes from the Old Testament, sometimes directly from the Hebrew (xiii. 18 ; xix. 37, etc.)

All that can be alleged against the apostolic authorship of the fourth Gospel, on account of its marked divergence from the other Gospels in the representation of Christ's character and teaching, is sufficiently met by the fact that "the synoptical Gospels contain the Gospel of the infant Church ; that of St. John, the Gospel in its maturity. The first combine to give the wide experience of the many ; the last embraces the deep mysteries treasured up by the one."[2] If we suppose the fourth Gospel to have been written about 85 A.D., an interval of more than half a century would thus have elapsed since the death of Christ. During that time Christianity had spread into many lands and furnished subjects for reflection to many minds, while the Jewish expectations and prejudices which had clung to many of the early members of the Church had been in a great measure dissipated by the fall of Jerusalem. In these circumstances it was inevitable that the truths of the Gospel should be viewed in new lights and assume more speculative forms ; and in Ephesus, as the great meeting-place of Oriental mysticism and Greek philosophy, the

---

[1] Speaking generally, we may say that it is to this Gospel we are chiefly indebted for our knowledge of the individualities of the apostles and other (minor) characters.

[2] Westcott's *Introduction to the Study of the Gospels*, p. 253.

deeper questions and more theological aspects of the new
religion would naturally claim a large measure of attention. (Cf. Paul's Epistles to the Colossians and the
Ephesians—Chaps. XV. and XVI.).

We thus see that, as the other Gospels had reference
to distinct types of thought for which they were severally
adapted, so the fourth Gospel was designed to meet the
demand for a more intellectual presentation of divine
truth, which might serve as an antidote to the Gnostic
speculations which were imperilling the recognition at
one time of Christ's divinity, and at another time of His
humanity. In God's providence a worthy exponent of
this phase of the Gospel was found in the aged Apostle
John, whose heart and mind had been so receptive of
divine truth even in his youth as to win for him the
place of closest fellowship with his Master, and who had
since then enjoyed the teaching of the Holy Spirit for a
longer period than any of his fellows, and amid more
intellectual surroundings, and was thus singularly fitted
for the great task which Providence had assigned to
him.[1]

2. Date of Composition.—85-90 A.D., as indicated
above.

3. Character and Contents.—Many of the remarks
that might have been made under this head have already
found place in this chapter, and in the general discussion
of the Gospels, where a contrast is drawn between the
Synoptics and the fourth Gospel. On the whole perhaps
no fitter epithet can be found for this Gospel than that

[1] The higher social position, and, presumably, better education,
of John and his brother (judging from his father's circumstances, his
personal acquaintance with the high priest, and his mother's request
for her two sons that they might sit the one on the right hand and the
other on the left hand of the Saviour in His kingdom) are perhaps not
without significance in this connection as helping to account for his
wider intellectual sympathies, which fitted him to be "the Plato of
the Twelve."

applied to it by Clement of Alexandria at the close of tho
second century, viz. the *spiritual* Gospel. It may also
be described as the *doctrinal* or *theological* Gospel. It
represents Christ's person and work not with special
reference to the Past, or the Present, or the Future;
but generally with reference to Eternity, in which Past,
Present, and Future are alike included.

Its great theme is set forth in the Prologue or Introduction (i. 1-18), which strikes the keynote of the whole
Gospel, representing Christ as the Manifestation of the
divine Being, the only Source of life and light, in human
form,[1] and, as such, the object, on the one hand, of
saving faith, and the occasion, on the other hand, of the
world's unbelief. The whole book is an elaboration of
this sublime thought, wrought out with a singular union
of depth and simplicity—in close historical relation with
the Lord's visits to Jerusalem at the national feasts, when
He had occasion to press His claims, as the Revealer of
the Father, upon the teachers of religion, in connection
with the national expectation of the Messiah. This
revelation, attested by various forms of divine witness-
bearing (including miracles, which are always called
"signs" in this Gospel, as expressions of Christ's glory),
may be said to reach a climax in xii. 37-40 ("These
things spake Jesus, and he departed and hid himself from
them. But though he had done so many signs before
them, yet they believed not on him.") The remainder
of the book depicts, on the one hand, the downward
course of the world's unbelief leading to the crucifixion,

---

[1] i. 1: "the Word was God." i. 14: "the Word became flesh."
It matters little how far the apostle was indebted to Philo or other
philosophising Jews for the use of the word "logos" as a term of
theology. In any case, he gave the word an entirely new application
by connecting it with the Incarnation, using it thus as a means of
bringing God nearer in a personal sense, instead of specu'ating about
Him in the region of an abstract theology.

and on the other, the perfecting of the disciples' faith, which attains its final and typical expression in the slowly-matured but deep-rooted confession of the doubting Thomas, "My Lord and my God" (xx. 28).

As already indicated, the fourth Gospel contains very few incidents of the ministry in Galilee. In this respect, as well as in many of its unexplained allusions (i. 32, 40; iii. 5, 13, 24; vi. 62, 70; xx. 17), it takes for granted acquaintance with the earlier Gospels.[1] The matter which it contains in common with the three other Gospels is very limited in extent, but of the most profound significance, viz. the Miraculous Feeding of the Multitude and the Death and Resurrection of Christ. A crucified and risen Saviour who can say of Himself, "I am the bread of life; he that cometh to me shall not hunger, and he that believeth on me shall never thirst,"—this is the essence of the four Gospels, as it is the essence of Christianity symbolised in the Lord's Supper; and the final object of the whole New Testament is summed up by the last of the apostles when he says, "These are written, that ye may believe that Jesus is the Christ, the Son of God; and that, believing, ye may have life in his name" (xx. 31).

---

[1] In keeping with this is the fact that many long intervals are passed over; *e.g.* between the feast of the Passover (vi. 4) and the feast of Tabernacles (vii. 2), during which time the evangelist expressly mentions that "Jesus walked in Galilee."

CHAPTER VII

"THE ACTS OF THE APOSTLES"

1. Authorship.—There can be no doubt that the Book of Acts is from the same pen as the third Gospel. This is evident from the preface at the head of each book, and from the general similarity of their style and structure.

An attempt has been made, however, to raise a distinction, as regards authorship, between different portions of the book. There are certain passages whose genuineness has scarcely ever been disputed—those, namely, in which the writer uses *the first person plural*, as having been himself present on the occasions referred to.[1] It is generally acknowledged that these passages are the genuine work of a companion of the apostle. But by a certain school of critics the rest of the book has a very different character assigned to it. According to them, the "we" passages formed the original notes of an eye-witness, which were made use of by a subsequent writer in the second century, as the nucleus of a history in

---

[1] From these passages it appears that the writer joined Paul's company at Troas (xvi. 10), that he accompanied him to Philippi, where he was left behind when Paul departed to another city, that after an interval of six or seven years he rejoined the apostle on the latter's return to Philippi, and accompanied him on his last journey to Jerusalem (xx. 5–xxi. 18), and afterwards from Cæsarea to Rome (xxvii. 1–xxviii. 16). Cf.-pp. 33-36.

great part fictitious, which was designed to bridge over the gulf between Paul and the rest of the apostles.

Even if this theory could be proved to be correct, it would not get rid of the supernatural element to which these critics have such an aversion, for in the passages thus admitted to be genuine there are statements that imply miraculous occurrences (xvi. 18, 26; xxviii. 8, 9).

But in reality there is no sufficient evidence to warrant such a view. With regard to external testimony, we find in some of the earliest Christian writers (Clement of Rome,[1] Ignatius, Polycarp, Hermas, Justin Martyr, etc.) not a few expressions which seem to reproduce the language of this book—drawn not only from the " we " sections but from other parts of it as well. The impression thus made upon us in favour of the book as it now stands is confirmed by finding it in the Syriac and Old Latin Versions, and also in the Muratorian Canon.

But it is the *internal* character of the book that affords the best refutation of the theory in question. A minute and critical examination of the account of Paul's missionary journeys before Luke joined him (Acts xiii., xiv.) has recently led an accomplished scholar and archæologist to the conclusion that it " is founded on, or perhaps actually incorporates, an account written down under the immediate influence of Paul himself."[2] Moreover, with a few exceptions, due to the variety of sources, oral or written, from which the author drew, the book has a natural unity of diction and style which forbids us to assign it to more than one author, and its several parts are so interlaced by corresponding observations and

---

[1] *E.g.* in his 1 Ep. xviii. there is a reproduction of Acts xiii. 22, in its combination of 1 Sam. xiii. 14 and Ps. lxxxix. 20, its addition of the phrase " son of Jesse," and its allusion to the divine *testimony*. In the Greek the resemblance is even more striking.

[2] Professor Ramsay, *The Church in the Roman Empire*, p. 6.

allusions as to confirm us in the belief that it forms one consistent whole.[1]

That it is a work of the first century may be inferred from the fact that it does not contain the slightest allusion to St. Paul's epistles. In the second century these epistles were so widely circulated that no historian giving a sketch of Paul's life-work could have passed them over in silence. But during the greater part of the period covered by the Book of Acts they were not yet in existence; and for some years they would be very little known except in the Churches to which they were addressed. There is no notice taken of them in the Book of Acts, nor is there any echo of their teaching; while there is a remarkable absence of information on several important points mentioned in them which would naturally have called for recognition had they been familiar to the writer of this book (*e.g.* Gal. i. 17; ii. 11; 2 Cor. xi. 24).

But although there is no sign of acquaintance with the epistles themselves, there are, as we shall see when we come to deal with these writings, many "*undesigned coincidences*" between statements contained in them and in the Book of Acts, which can only be accounted for by the fact that the writers, in both cases, were guided by a strict regard for truth.

It has also to be noted that while there is no sign of acquaintance with Paul's letters, there is in the speeches attributed to him an admitted resemblance to his style and diction, which is best accounted for by the writer's having been present at the delivery of the speeches, or

[1] Cf. vi. 5, viii. 40, xxi. 8; vii. 58, viii. 1, xxii. 20; i. 5, xi. 16 (a saying of our Lord's being here twice quoted which does not occur in any of the four Gospels); x. 47, xv. 8; ix. 30, xi. 25, etc. In *The Expositor* of January 1894 Professor Ramsay says: "The more closely Acts is scrutinised, the more clearly do the unity and first-hand character of the narrative stand out."

having received an authentic report of them. It is interesting in this connection to observe that the speech which Paul delivered in Hebrew on the stairs of the castle in Jerusalem (xxii. 1-21), and which was no doubt translated into its present Greek form by Luke (judging from the number of Luke's favourite words to be found in it), is far less Pauline in character than the speech at Athens (xvii. 22-31), which was spoken in Greek, and was in all probability reported to Luke by Paul himself. We may add that this latter speech is not only Pauline in its diction, but reflects very plainly the apostle's training in the schools of Tarsus, where the Stoic philosophy was in great repute. We have a similar token of genuineness in the harmony between the speeches of Peter reported in this book and the first epistle written by that apostle.[1]

Of the writer's accuracy in matters of fact abundant evidence can be adduced. In the titles which he gives to the magistrates of the various cities he has occasion to mention, he is supported by the testimony of ancient writings, coins, and inscriptions in a most remarkable manner; *e.g.* the name of politarchs ("rulers of the city"), which he applies to the magistrates of Thessalonica (xvii. 6), though otherwise unknown, has been discovered on an arch still in comparatively good preservation in the principal street of the city.[2] His many allusions also to historical characters and conditions that are otherwise known to us, are almost invariably found to be true to fact;[3] while the precision of his *nautical*

---

[1] Cf. ii. 23, iv. 28, and 1 Peter i. 2, 20 ; also iv. 11 and 1 Peter ii. 4-8.

[2] Similar instances are found at xiii. 7 ; xvi. 12, 20 ; xviii. 12 ; xxviii. 7. See Salmon's *Introduction*, pp. 348, 349.

[3] For example, Professor Ramsay remarks that the importance assigned to the south Galatian Churches, in chaps. xiii., xiv., "is historically true to the period 48-64 A.D. and not to later time." Referring to the story of the tumult in the temple of Diana, the same

expressions and minute *geographical* allusions in his account of Paul's voyage and shipwreck, has been found so remarkable as to form the subject of a special dissertation.[1]

As a last token of genuineness may be mentioned the fact that in the Book of Acts the positions taken up by the Pharisees and Sadducees respectively with reference to Christ's cause are almost *the reverse of what they are in the Gospel*. This change of attitude was due to the apostles' preaching of the Resurrection, after their Master's departure, which was fitted to give offence to the Sadducees alone ; but it is a circumstance which only a contemporary would have been likely to realise and represent in such a vivid manner.

2. Date of Composition.—With regard to the date of its composition, its abrupt termination—leaving us in ignorance of Paul's fate and of his subsequent labours (if he was set free from his imprisonment at Rome)—has led some to suppose that the author brought up his narrative to the very moment when he closed the book and despatched it to his friend Theophilus. In that case it must have left the writer's hands about 63 A.D. But it may be that the work was broken off owing to Luke's death, or he may have had it in view to complete his narrative in another volume, or he may have felt it dangerous to go farther. Yet another view is that the apostle's preaching at Rome was purposely selected by the writer as a suitable finish to his narrative of the Church's progress. On the whole, we may be content with the assurance that it was written by a contemporary and companion of the apostle.

writer says, " There is only one way of interpreting it, and that is as embodying almost, if not absolutely, *verbatim*, the words of an eye-witness."

[1] *Voyage and Shipwreck of St. Paul*, by James Smith, Esq., F.R.S., of Jordanhill.

3. Character and Contents.—The *keynote* of the book is struck in the commission given by the risen Lord to His apostles (i. 8): "But ye shall receive power, when the Holy Ghost is come upon you: and ye shall be my witnesses, both in Jerusalem, and in all Judæa, and Samaria, and unto the uttermost part of the earth." The entire book records the fulfilment of this prophecy. It may be roughly divided into three parts corresponding to the widening spheres of labour which were thus indicated—"Jerusalem" (i. 13-vii.); "all Judæa and Samaria" (viii.-ix); "unto the uttermost part of the earth" (x.-xxviii.) Each of the three is marked by a notable outpouring of the Holy Spirit (ii. 1-4; viii. 17; x. 44-48).

Throughout the whole narrative *prominence is given to the Lord Jesus Christ*, as the subject of apostolic testimony (ii. 32; iii. 13-15; v. 31, 32, 42; viii. 5; x. 36-42), as the bestower of the Holy Spirit (ii. 33), with His miraculous gifts (iii. 16; ix. 34) and divine guidance (i. 24; x. 19; xvi. 6-10), as personally visible to the martyr Stephen (vii. 56), and as the personal agent in Paul's conversion (ix. 3-5).

There is great significance in the description of Luke's Gospel, given in the opening verse of this book, as a treatise "concerning all that Jesus *began* both to do and to teach, until the day in which he was received up." The position of the word "began" is very emphatic in the original, as if to imply that the Acts of the Apostles formed a continuation of Christ's work. The writer conceives of Him as still carrying on His work in virtue of His Resurrection and Ascension; and in the introduction to the book he refers to these events as well as to the prediction of His second Advent (i. 1-11).

The continuity of the divine work is indeed *the ruling idea* of the whole book. The Gospel kingdom is described as advancing steadily onwards, beginning at Jerusalem (in the same upper room, perhaps, as had been the scene of the Last Supper), and extending finally to Rome, the great metropolis of the Gentiles. More than half the book is devoted to the labours of the Apostle of the Gentiles, and three of his missionary journeys are recorded—with Antioch for his headquarters, where the "disciples were first called Christians" (xi. 26).

Of necessity it is a mere *selection* of incidents that is given, both as regards the labours of Paul (cf. 2 Cor. xi. 24-27), and the history of the Church during the thirty-three years or more over which the book extends. The selection was no doubt determined partly by the information which Luke had gathered from his own observation as an eye-witness or from trustworthy reporters,[1] and partly by the great object he had in view, namely, to trace the gradual expansion of the Church from its first beginnings[2] as a seeming phase of Judaism to its full development as a catholic communion, in which there was to be no distinction between Jew and Gentile, and where the Law, on which the former prided himself so greatly, was to be superseded by the *grace*[3] of God freely offered in the Gospel.

---

[1] *E.g.* the account of the mission in Samaria and elsewhere in chap. viii. would, no doubt, be mainly derived from Philip, with whom the writer (xxi. 8-10) had spent many days at Cæsarea, which had also been the scene of the notable events relating to the admission of Cornelius the centurion, recorded in chap. x.

[2] "It tells us of the first apostolic miracle; the first apostolic sermon; the first beginnings of ecclesiastical organisation; the first persecution; the first martyr; the first Gentile convert; the first ecclesiastical synod; the first mission journey; the first European church" (Farrar, *Messages of the Books*).

[3] A favourite word both with St. Luke and St. Paul.

CHAPTER VIII

The Epistles of St. Paul—His Previous History

1. The Epistles.—One of the distinguishing characteristics of the New Testament as compared with all other
sacred books in the world is the *epistolary* character of a
large part of its contents.

It contains twenty-one letters by six different authors.
Nine of these are addressed to individual Churches, viz.
1 and 2 Thessalonians, 1 and 2 Corinthians, Galatians,
Romans, Philippians, Colossians, 2 John (see chap. xxiii.);
five to individual persons, viz. Philemon, 1 and 2 Timothy,
Titus, 3 John; and two to Hebrew Christians, viz.
Hebrews and James; the remaining five being of a more
or less general nature, viz. Ephesians (see chap. xvi.),
1 and 2 Peter, 1 John, and Jude.

Besides these, we have reason to believe from the
nature of the case (2 Cor. xi. 28), as well as from special
allusions (1 Cor. v. 9; 2 Thess. iii. 17), that there were
other apostolic letters which have not been preserved.
That Providence should have suffered such inspired
writings to perish is in no degree more remarkable than
that so many of our Lord's own words should have passed
into oblivion; and we can readily understand that during

the apostles' lifetime their letters were less prized than after their death, when the loss of any of their writings was seen to be irreparable.

Although most of the epistles were written at an earlier period than the Gospels, they represent in general a more advanced stage of Christian theology. In the epistles we have the fruits of twenty to fifty years' reflection on the great facts and elementary truths contained in the Synoptical Gospels, viewed in the light of Christian experience and under the teaching of the Holy Spirit, taking of the things that are Christ's and showing them to the Church. To the epistles we are mainly indebted for our knowledge of Christian doctrine on such subjects as the Trinity, the relations of Christ to the human race and to His Church, the Atonement, Justification by Faith, and Sanctification by the Holy Spirit.

But while largely doctrinal in character, most of the epistles differ very considerably from formal treatises, being enlivened with personal allusions, and dealing largely with questions of a practical nature.

2. The Epistles of St. Paul.—The remark just made applies specially to the epistles of Paul, which had their rise not in abstract speculations, but in the special needs and circumstances of the various Churches to which they were addressed. They are filled with the living personality of the writer, and lay hold so vividly upon the reader's sympathies, that they have been described by Luther as "not mere dead words, but living creatures with hands and feet."

They are thirteen in number. Their composition ranges over a period of about fifteen years, the earliest of them (1 and 2 Thess.) having been written about 53 A.D., at least sixteen years after the apostle's conversion ; the last of them (the Pastoral Epistles to Titus and

Timothy) very near the close of his life, approaching 68 A.D.

In the interval were produced two other groups of epistles—those designed to vindicate Paul's apostolic authority, and preserve the Gospel from the inroads of Judaism, viz. 1 and 2 Corinthians, Galatians, and Romans (written during his third missionary journey, about 57-58 A.D.), and the Epistles of the Imprisonment, viz. Philippians, Colossians, Philemon, and Ephesians, written from Rome about 62-63 A.D.

The most of them were probably collected and in more or less general use in the Church within a short time after the apostle's death, as we may infer from the traces of them to be found in the writings of Clement of Rome (95 A.D.), Ignatius (died 110-115 A.D.), and Poly-carp (wrote 110-115 A.D., died 155-156 A.D.).

In our New Testament the Pauline epistles are ar-ranged according to their length and importance, but there is an obvious advantage in studying them in their *chronological order*, as it enables us to trace the progres-sive development of the apostle's theology and the growth of his literary style, as well as to realise the circumstances out of which the epistles successively arose.

It is a circumstance worth noting as an explanation in some measure of the occasional abruptness and irregu-larity of the apostle's style (and perhaps of its vivacity), that his letters were usually written by an amanuensis to dictation,—the salutation only being written with his own hand, as a token of genuineness.[1]

3. **The undisputed Epistles of St. Paul.**—1 and 2 Corinthians, Romans, and Galatians have the distinction of being almost universally admitted to be genuine writings of Paul.

[1] Cf. Rom. xvi. 22 ; 1 Cor. xvi. 21 and Col. iv. 18 ; Gal. vi. 11 ; 2 Thess. iii. 17 ; Philemon, ver. 19.

This admission is a most important one from an *evidential* point of view, as these epistles form a valuable historical link between the earliest preaching of the apostles and the composition of our four Gospels. They contain a great many references to detailed matters of fact mentioned in the Gospels, and prove that the story of Christ's death and resurrection, as told in the four Gospels, was the chief theme of Paul's preaching (1 Cor. xv. 1-8; xi. 23-28).

With regard to our Lord's resurrection in particular, they prove that event to have been generally believed in by the Church in St. Paul's time, and to have been from the first the basis of the apostle's preaching (1 Cor. xv. 1-20). They also imply the exercise of supernatural powers by the apostle himself, as a fact generally admitted and not likely to be called in question even by those who were opposed to him (2 Cor. xii. 11-13), and they show the existence in the Church of spiritual gifts on a large scale and with many well-defined variations, that were commonly regarded as the result of supernatural influence (1 Cor. xii.-xiv.).

We are thus in a great measure independent of the four Gospels for our knowledge of the original truths and principles of Christianity; and we have in the epistles a practical refutation of the mythical theories which would attribute the supernatural elements in our Gospels to the gradual growth of legend in the Church.

The evidence derived from the epistles is all the more valuable because it is indirect, the letters having manifestly been written without any such object in view. It has to be noted too that they are addressed to several independent communities far removed from one another. One of these communities (the Church in Rome) had received its Christianity from another source than the apostle, while in the two others (Corinth and Galatia)

there were opponents to criticise his statements, as well
as friends to sympathise with him.   In these circumstances falsehood or error with reference to important
matters of fact was extremely improbable.   To this we
may add that the letters are evidently the productions
of a man whose sincerity is as great as his intellectual
acuteness and sobriety of judgment, and who, from his
early association with the Jewish authorities at Jerusalem,
was in a position to know all that could be said against
the alleged facts of Christianity.

Altogether, it is not too much to say that a study
of these epistles leads inevitably to the conclusion that
Paul's gospel had the same historical groundwork as the
gospel preached at the present day—that groundwork
consisting of the same essential and well-attested facts
regarding Christ's life and teaching as we find recorded
in the four Gospels.

4. St. Paul's previous History.—Regarding the pre·
vious life of the author, the following brief statement may
suffice.   Paul (originally called Saul) was born within a
few years after our Lord's nativity, in the city of Tarsus
in Cilicia, a famous seat of classical learning.   His father,
though a Roman citizen, was of Hebrew descent, and
brought up his son in the strictest observance of the
Jewish law.   Trained at Jerusalem under the renowned
Pharisaic teacher Gamaliel, Saul became thoroughly
versed in Rabbinical literature, and was equally distinguished for his learning and his zeal.   He was among
the earliest and fiercest persecutors of the Christians,
whom he regarded as apostates from the religion of their
fathers; and it was while he was on his way to Damascus
in the execution of a warrant from the high priest that
he was suddenly converted (34-37 A.D.) by the direct
interposition of the Risen Christ.   From Him he received
a special commission to preach the Gospel to the Gentiles,

and in His service he continued with unflinching courage and devotion, in spite of calumny and persecution, to the last hour of his life. After about eight years, spent partly in retirement, partly in preaching in Syria and Cilicia, he joined (about 44 A.D.) his old friend Barnabas, a liberal - minded evangelist or "apostle," at Antioch, which was soon to become the great centre of missionary enterprise for the early Church. In company with Barnabas, Paul made his first missionary journey (about 48 A.D.), through Cyprus and part of Asia Minor, and attended the Council at Jerusalem (about 50 A.D.), to advocate the cause of the Gentile converts in their struggle against the bigotry of their Jewish brethren. In the following year he started on his second and more extensive missionary tour, in the course of which, under the divine guidance, he crossed over to Europe, founding a number of Churches there, among others that of Thessalonica. He reached Corinth in 52 A.D., from which, as we shall presently see, he wrote the first of his epistles that have been preserved to us, namely 1 and 2 Thessalonians.

CHAPTER IX

1 AND 2 THESSALONIANS

"THE FIRST EPISTLE OF PAUL THE APOSTLE TO THE THESSALONIANS"

1. Authorship.—There is ample external evidence to prove that this epistle was acknowledged to be a genuine writing of St. Paul in the second quarter of the second century, while expressions apparently borrowed from it are to be found in writings of a still earlier date.

The few critics, headed by Baur, who have called its genuineness in question have done so on internal grounds, alleging against it both its likeness and its unlikeness to the other epistles of Paul. But its unlikeness is satisfactorily accounted for by the comparatively early date of its composition, and the very exceptional nature of the occasion on which it was written; while its likeness is largely due to the habit of repetition which is a marked characteristic of the apostle, and, in particular, to the germination, at this early period, of ideas more fully developed in his subsequent writings. Moreover, the resemblance between this and other writings of St. Paul is often so subtle and minute—depending on the play of personal feeling and affection for his converts,[1] or on

[1] Cf. ii. 17-20, iii. 6-10, and Rom. i. 13, 2 Cor. i. 16, xiii. 1.

characteristic peculiarities of style,[1]—as to preclude the idea of forgery.

The language of the epistle with reference to the Second Coming of Christ is also at variance with the supposition of forgery. It seems to imply an expectation on the part of the apostle that he would live to see that event (iv. 15-17). But such an expectation was not likely to be introduced by a forger when it had already been falsified by the apostle's death,—as it must have been, long before forgery could have been successfully attempted. In this connection we may also note the apparent discrepancy between the statements in Acts xviii. 5 and 1 Thess. i. 3 regarding the movements of Timothy, into which a forger depending for his informa-. tion on the Book of Acts would not have been likely to fall, and which can only be accounted for by supposing a journey of Timothy (from Athens or Berœa to Thessalonica) left unrecorded in the Book of Acts. There is a similar discrepancy between chapter i. 9, which speaks of the converts as having "turned from their idols," and Acts xvii. 4, as the latter would lead us to suppose that the Church of Thessalonica was largely composed of Jews and proselytes.[2] In ii. 17, 18 there is a reference to the apostle's disappointment in not being able to carry out his intention of revisiting his converts, but such an intention is nowhere mentioned in the Book of Acts. All the three variations may be regarded as a proof that the epistle

[1] *E.g.* a cursory sequence of thought (i. 2-8) ; the combination of seeming contraries (i. 6, cf. 2 Cor. viii. 1, Col. i. 11, 12); verbal contrasts (ii. 17 ; iv. 7, cf. 1 Cor. v. 3, 2 Cor. v. 1, 2). The force of these arguments cannot be fully understood without a knowledge of the original (Jowett, vol. i. pp. 19-25).

[2] The difficulty may be met by adopting a reading of Acts xvii. 4 that is found in some MSS. and is followed in the Vulgate, namely, "of the devout (proselytes) and the Greeks a great multitude," or by supposing that the apostle preached to the Gentiles after the three Sabbath-days mentioned in Acts xvii. 2.

was written independently of the Acts, and that their general harmony is due to their common fidelity to facts.

2. The Readers.—" Unto the Church of the Thessalonians." Thessalonica was then, as it is still (under the name of Saloniki), an important mercantile emporium, at the head of the Thermaic Gulf, with a considerable proportion of Jewish inhabitants sharing in its general prosperity. It is now the second city of European Turkey ; in the time of the apostle it was the capital of Macedonia. It lay in the neighbourhood of Mount Olympus, the fabled home of the gods, and was a place of exile for Cicero, who tells how he gazed up at the sacred summit but saw nothing save snow and ice.

The Church of Thessalonica was planted by St. Paul in the course of his second missionary tour in 52 A.D. (Acts xvii. 1-11), after his memorable visit to Philippi. His stay in Thessalonica seems to have been short, owing to a rising of the mob, stirred up against him by the Jews ; but it was long enough for the Philippians to send " once and again " unto his need (Phil. iv. 16). Previously he had been earning his own bread (ii. 9 ; 2 Thess. iii. 7, 8)—doubtless in the exercise of his calling as a tentmaker (Acts xviii. 3), as "one of the staple manufactures of the city was and is goats'-hair cloth. The sound that follows the ear as one walks through the streets of Saloniki to-day is the wheezing and straining vibration of the loom and the pendulum-like click of the regular and ceaseless shuttle." [1]   Paul paid a second visit to the place shortly before his last journey to Jerusalem. The Church was mainly Gentile, as we may infer not only from its members having "turned unto God from idols" (i. 9), but also from the fact that the epistles addressed to it do not contain a single quotation from the Old Testament.

Thessalonica played a great part in the history of

---

[1] Dods' *Introduction to the New Testament*, p. 153.

Christendom, as a bulwark against the Turks, whence it was known as the Orthodox city. Its modern population (about 90,000) consists chiefly of Mohammedans and Jews, and includes but a small number of Christians.

3. Date and Place of Composition.—The epistle itself supplies us with an answer. From iii. 6-8 we learn that it was written on the return of Timothy, whom Paul had sent (apparently from Athens) to revisit the Thessalonian Church (iii. 1, 2). But Acts xviii. 5 informs us that Silas and Timothy rejoined the apostle during his stay of a year and a half at Corinth. We conclude therefore that the epistle was written from that city,—not long after the apostle's arrival, as we may infer from his language in 'ii. 17 : " But we, brethren, being bereaved of you for a short season, in presence, not in heart." This would be about 53 A.D., probably early in that year.

4. Character and Contents.—This epistle is an outpouring of the apostle's feelings towards a Church whose hearty reception of the Gospel was to him a matter of constant gratitude to God (i. 2-6), from which he had been reluctantly separated (ii. 17 ; iii. 1, 2), whose reputation (owing to the constant traffic of the city both by land and sea) had already spread far and wide (i. 7-10), and of whose patience and constancy he had received a gratifying report from Timothy (iii. 6-9). It contains also a vindication of his own character from the aspersions of the Jews, who were imputing to him the basest motives, and seem in particular to have put a bad construction on his sudden departure from the city. In refutation of these calumnies Paul appeals to the experience his converts had of his life and conduct while he was with them, and to the salutary effects of his preaching (ii.) After telling of the yearning anxiety he had felt on their account, and of the joy which Timothy's report had given him, he prays that God would grant him a fulfilment of the desire, which he feels intensely, to re-visit them for the perfecting of "that which is lacking in (their) faith," and that meanwhile their spiritual life may be developed and strengthened (iii 10-13). With this view he exhorts them (iv.) to the cultivation of certain virtues—purity (vv. 1-8), brotherly love (vv. 9, 10), industry (vv. 11, 12)—which they were in danger of neglecting.

The characteristic feature of this epistle, however, as of that which follows, is the prominence it gives to Christ's Second Coming. This had been a main theme of Paul's preaching when he was in Thessalonica (i. 10; ii. 12; cf. Acts xvii. 7), and it had so taken possession of his hearers that the bereavements they had suffered by the death of relatives since the apostle left them, were chiefly mourned because they thought the departed friends would have no share in the glory of the Saviour's Advent. The comfort which Paul administers (iv. 13-18) when he assures his converts that their fears in this matter are groundless, gives one the idea that he expected Christ to come in his own lifetime. In this respect the language of this epistle differs widely from the allusions to his approaching death in his later epistles (2 Cor. v. 1; Phil. i. 21-24; 2 Tim. iv. 6). That the apostle should have been left to his own impressions in this matter is in striking harmony with our Lord's statement, "But of that day and hour knoweth no one, not even the angels of heaven, neither the Son, but the Father only" (Matt. xxiv. 36, cf. Acts i. 7). That it would come suddenly and called for constant watchfulness was a truth often dwelt upon by Christ, which the apostle could safely enforce, as he does in this epistle (v. 1-11).[1]

---

[1] With regard to the arrangement of topics in this the earliest of Paul's writings that has come down to us, we can trace the order that may be said to be characteristic of his epistles generally, viz.: (1) Salutation, (2) Thanksgiving and Prayer, (3) Doctrinal Instruction, (4) Practical Exhortation, (5) Personal Messages, (6) Concluding Salutation and Benediction.

"THE SECOND EPISTLE OF PAUL THE APOSTLE TO THE THESSALONIANS"

1. Authorship.—We have the same external evidence for the genuineness of the second epistle as of the first. Internally it bears evidence of being a sequel to the other, being written, like it, in the name of Paul and Silas and Timothy (i. 1), and containing a direct allusion to the previous epistle (ii. 15). As might have been expected, it contains fewer and more distant allusions to the apostle's sojourn in Thessalonica, although it expressly recalls the teaching he had then imparted regarding the revelation of "the man of sin." As regards style and language it exhibits many Pauline peculiarities in common with the first epistle.

The prophetic passage in chapter ii. 1-12 has been a stumbling-block to many critics, who have imagined it to bear the stamp of a later period. In reality, however, it is quite consistent with the teaching of the first epistle, which nowhere implies that the coming of Christ was to be immediate, although it was to be sudden and was apparently to take place in the apostle's lifetime. Predictions of a similar kind had been uttered by our Lord Himself (Matt. xxiv.), and were also to be found in the books of Daniel and Ezekiel.

2. The Readers.—See page 66.

3. Date and Place of Composition.—As above remarked, this epistle, like the first, is written in the name of Paul, Silas, and Timothy. The three were together at Corinth, and apparently, so far as the Book of Acts informs us, nowhere else. This leads to the inference that this epistle, like the first, was written from that city—probably a few months later. In the interval the excitement and disorder at Thessalonica consequent upon the expectation of Christ's coming, in the midst of the perse-cution to which the converts were exposed, had grown even more serious, and demanded the apostle's attention (i. 5 ; ii. 6 ; iii. 6-11).

4. Character and Contents.—Along with an expression of satisfaction with their continued faith and steadfastness in the midst of their persecutions and afflictions (i. 1-4), Paul assures the Thessalonians that Christ will infallibly come to vindicate their cause, "rendering vengeance" to His and their enemies, and at the same time "to be glorified in his saints" (i. 5-12). But he warns them against being carried away with the idea—due in some measure to a misconstruction of his own teaching or to the circulation of a forged epistle bearing his name (ii. 1, 2 ; iii. 17)—that Christ's coming was immediately to take place. He mentions that certain great events must first come to pass (ii. 3-12), and exhorts them to the exercise of continued patience in the strength of divine grace (ii. 13-17), bidding them lead a quiet, honest, and in-dustrious life, such as he had given an example of while he was yet with them, and commanding them to "withdraw (themselves) from every brother that walketh disorderly" (iii. 6-16).

The characteristic passage of the epistle is that which deals with "the falling away" that must "come first" before Christ's appearing (ii. 1-12). Its meaning has been the subject of endless controversy, owing to the attempts which have been made to identify the "man of sin," and the "one that restraineth now," with historical dynasties or persons. For the former there have been suggested Nero, Mahomet, the Pope, Luther, Napoleon ; for the latter the Roman Empire, the German Empire, Claudius, and even Paul himself. But the truer inter-pretation seems to be to regard the expressions in question as referring to two great tendencies—the one

antichristian, in the form of secular ambition, which was
all that the hope of a Messiah then amounted to in many
Jewish minds, and the other political, in the form of
the civil power, represented in the first instance by the
Roman Empire. The breakdown of the civil power before
the aggressive march of an ungodly Socialism, under the
leadership perhaps of some one realising on a gigantic
scale the antichristian feeling and ambition of the age,
may be the signal for the Advent of the true Christ in
His heavenly power and glory.[1]

[1] The obscurity of the passage is partly due to its prophetic
character, partly to the need for caution in any references to the
interests of the state, and partly to the fact that the apostle takes for
granted the personal instruction he had already given to the Thessalonians on the same subject.

CHAPTER X

"THE FIRST EPISTLE OF PAUL THE APOSTLE TO THE CORINTHIANS"

1. Authorship.—As already mentioned, the Pauline authorship of this epistle is admitted with practical unanimity. The external evidence is abundant, from the end of the first century onward. In particular we find in the first epistle of Clement of Rome to the Church of Corinth (95 A.D.) the following unmistakable reference: "Take up the epistle of the blessed Paul the apostle. What was it that he first wrote to you in the beginning of the gospel? Of a truth it was under the influence of the Spirit that he wrote to you in his epistle concerning himself and Cephas and Apollos, because then as well as now you had formed partialities" (cf. 1 Cor. i. 12).

But the internal evidence would of itself be decisive. For this epistle—and still more 2 Corinthians—bears very distinct traces of the opposition which Paul had to encounter before his apostolic authority was firmly established ; and we know that such opposition had been vanquished long before his death. It is full of minute references to the state of the Corinthian Church—being to a large extent the apostle's reply to a letter of inquiry from that Church (vii. 1), although it also deals with a number of evils and disorders in the Church which, it appears, had come to the apostle's knowledge through other channels (i. 11; v. 1; xi. 18). This last circumstance, as Paley points out in his *Horœ Paulinœ* (iii. 1), is a token of historical reality, as it is not likely that the Corinthians would deliberately expose their own faults. Indeed their very acknowledgment and preservation of the epistle, notwithstanding the aspersions which it casts on their early character as a Church, is a proof of its apostolic claims to their regard. It is worthy of remark, too, that it contains numerous references to Paul's movements, which would scarcely have been ventured on by an impostor; and a comparison of the epistle with the Book of Acts and other parts of the New Testament brings out many striking coincidences, which can best be accounted for on the supposition of its genuineness.[1]

Along with Paul Sosthenes is associated in the opening verse (possibly the converted ruler of the synagogue, Acts xviii. 17). He may have acted as the apostle's amanuensis.

2. The Readers.—"Unto the church of God which is at Corinth" (i. 2). In the apostle's time Corinth was practically the capital of Greece. It had attained pre-eminence at a much earlier period, owing to its commercial advantages, but had been destroyed by the Roman conqueror about two hundred years before Paul's visit. After lying in ruins for a century, it was rebuilt by Julius Cæsar 46 B.C., and peopled by a Roman colony. This may account for the Roman names mentioned in the epistle (i. 14; xvi. 17). We have an allusion to the effects produced by the ravages of the conqueror on the various kinds of buildings (iii. 12, 13), and also to the gladiatorial exhibitions (iv. 9).

Situated at the foot of a great rock called Acrocorinthus about 2000 feet high on the Isthmus (famous for

---

[1] Cf. iii. 6 and Acts xviii. 24, xix. 1; xvi. 10, 11, Acts xix. 21, 22 and 1 Tim. iv. 12; i. 14-17, xvi. 15, Acts xviii. 8 and Rom. xvi. 23.

its games, ix. 24-27) which connected the Peloponnesus
with the mainland, and lying in the direct route between
Ephesus and Rome, Corinth rapidly regained its former
prosperity, and became the chief emporium of Europe,[1]
with a population of more than half a million, drawn
from many lands. It was so notorious for its profligacy—
encouraged by its very worship—that a "Corinthian
life" was synonymous with luxury and licentiousness. At
the same time its inhabitants made such pretensions to
philosophical and literary culture that "Corinthian
words" was a phrase meaning polished and cultivated
speech.

In this great and busy centre Paul spent a year and
a half or more (Acts xviii.) in his second missionary
journey—being the longest time he had ever yet laboured
continuously in any city. He found a home in the
house of Aquila and Priscilla, a Jewish couple who had
recently come from Rome in consequence of the decree
of Claudius (xvi. 19), eminent for their generosity and
devotion (Rom. xvi. 4, 5); and with them he wrought at
his trade of tent-making (Acts xviii. 2, 3; xx. 34, 35;
1 Cor. iv. 11, 12).

Beginning his ministry in the synagogue as usual, he
was soon compelled by the opposition of the Jews to
seek another place of meeting, which he found in the
house of Justus, a converted proselyte. There he
preached the Gospel, encouraged by a message from God
in a vision, and continued to do so with no small success
notwithstanding an attempt of the Jews to invoke the
civil power against him (Acts xviii. 4-18). His converts
appear to have been chiefly drawn from the lower classes
(i. 26-29), but they were not free from the prevailing

---

[1] It had two harbours, Eastern and Western, named Cenchreæ and
Lechæum. A few years after the apostle's visit Nero cut the first
turf for a canal across the Isthmus; but the project was not carried
out.

tendency to intellectual pride (i. 17–ii. 1–f.; viii. 1),
accompanied with a proneness to sensual sin, equally
characteristic of their city (v. 1-11; vi. 15-18; xi. 21).
The apostle speaks (ii. 3) of having been with them "in
weakness and in fear, and in much trembling"—possibly
the result of his recent apparent failure at Athens.

3. Date and Place of Composition.—It can be proved
with tolerable certainty that the epistle was written from
Ephesus[1] about the spring of 57 A.D.

From iv. 17-19 and xvi. 5 we learn that it was
written on the eve of a second visit to Corinth, which
the apostle was about to pay after passing through Macedonia,—having already sent Timothy in advance as his
representative (xvi. 10). When we turn to the Book of
Acts we find that such a visit to Greece was paid by the
apostle at the close of a sojourn of about three years at
Ephesus (Acts xix. 8-10; xx. 1-3, 31), and it appears
from xix. 21-23 that almost immediately before he left
Ephesus he sent Timothy before him to Macedonia.
Moreover, several expressions in the epistle plainly point
to Ephesus as the place from which it emanated (xvi.
8-10, cf. Acts xix. 20-26; xvi. 19, cf. Acts xviii. 18-26;
xv. 32).

As the apostle appears to have travelled for about a
year after leaving Corinth on the first occasion (54 A.D.),
previous to settling at Ephesus, his stay in the latter
city may have extended to the beginning of 58 A.D.
Several allusions to the seasons, which occur in the epistle
(v. 7, 8; xvi. 6, 8), lead us to place its composition in the
spring of 57 A.D.

4. Character and Contents.—Of this epistle it has

---

[1] The note at the end of the epistle in the A.V. is due to a
misapprehension of xvi. 5 ("But I will come unto you, when I shall
have passed through Macedonia; for I do pass through Macedonia"),
as if it implied that Paul was passing through Macedonia when he
wrote the epistle.

been fitly said that it is "a fragment which has no parallel in ecclesiastical history." It deals with a section of early Church history which exhibits the most marked and varied features. It sets the apostle vividly before us as a teacher and governor, confronted with the dangers and perplexities, the errors and corruptions to which the Corinthian Church was liable, planted as it was in the midst of the rankest heathenism. In the words of Dean Stanley, "we are here allowed to witness the earliest conflict of Christianity with the culture and the vices of the ancient classical world; here we have an insight into the principles which regulated the apostle's choice or rejection of the customs of that vast fabric of heathen society which was then emphatically called 'the world'; here we trace the mode in which he combated the false pride, the false knowledge, the false liberality, the false freedom, the false display, the false philosophy, to which an intellectual age, especially in a declining nation, is constantly liable."

The epistle is thus eminently practical, dealing with questions that had actually emerged in the experience of the Church to which it is addressed. In form it is orderly and logical, taking up one point after another in regular succession; in style it is more simple and direct than most of Paul's compositions, rising at times into the sublimest eloquence, as in the great eulogium on love in the 13th chapter.

As already mentioned, the epistle was in part the reply to a letter of inquiry which had been sent to the apostle by the Corinthian Church in consequence of a letter which he had previously addressed to them (v. 9-11; vii. 1; xvi. 17, 18).

But the first six chapters have mainly reference to certain dangers threatening the Church, of which information had reached the apostle from another quarter,

causing him the utmost anxiety and grief (2 Cor. ii. 4).
These dangers were mainly twofold—the prevalence of
party spirit, and the tendency to immorality. Hence
the prominence given, in the opening salutation, to the
holiness to which Christians are called, and to their
unity in Christ; hence, too, the fact that in the accompanying thanksgiving for tokens of grace in the Corinthian Church, it is gifts of knowledge and utterance
rather than graces of character that are specially mentioned.

(1) The tendency to sectarian division mentioned in
i. 12 seems to have been fostered by emissaries from
Jerusalem, who wished to undermine Paul's authority,
and wrought upon the feelings and prejudices of the
Jewish portion of the Church (ix. 1-5; 2 Cor.). The
visit of Apollos, a learned and eloquent Jew of Alexandria, after Paul's departure (Acts xviii. 27, 28), had
tended in the same direction, by leading to an invidious
comparison between his philosophical and rhetorical style
of preaching and the more simple method of Paul, although the latter continued to regard him as a valuable
coadjutor (xvi. 12). But there were some—probably the
Judaising party—who were content neither with the
teaching of Paul nor of Apollos, but were disposed
to range themselves under the name and authority of
Cephas, as the leader of the twelve apostles and an
observer of the Law. Others professed to be independent
of human teachers, and claimed a more direct connection
with Christ, probably through their personal acquaintance with "the brethren of the Lord" (ix. 5), or their
national and historical affinity with Christ. In opposition to all these divisive courses, the apostle insists on the
supremacy of Christ as the one Lord and Saviour. He
introduces His name more frequently in this epistle than
in any other of his writings (nine times, for example, in

the first nine verses), and represents himself and other apostles as being not the heads of different schools, but simply the ministers of Christ, by whom their converts were brought to a knowledge of the truth as it is in Jesus.

(2) With regard to the immorality invading the Church, the apostle begins by referring to a terrible scandal—the taking to wife by a Christian of his stepmother during his father's lifetime (v. 1-5, cf. 2 Cor. vii. 12). In the exercise of his apostolic authority he pronounces a stern sentence on the offender, and urges the necessity for an uncompromising opposition to all such sin, and separation from those guilty of it, if they be members of the Church (chap. v.). In the next chapter, after deprecating the bringing of legal actions by Christians against one another in the heathen courts, he rebukes the Antinomian tendencies among them, and lays down the fundamental principles on which the Christian law of purity must rest.

The apostle then proceeds to answer the inquiries of his converts on the subject of marriage and celibacy, distinguishing between his own personal views and the expressed will of Christ (vii.). In viii.-x. he deals with what was to his readers a subject of vast importance— the duty of Christians with reference to the feasts that were held in the idol temples, and more particularly with regard to the use of the flesh of animals offered in sacrifice, which was almost the only kind of animal food that could be bought in the market. This question he bids them consider not in the abstract, but as it bears on the interests of Christian society, and as it is likely to affect not only their own character but the character and feelings of their fellow-Christians. In this connection he cites his own example of self-denial even in things lawful. In xi.-xiv. he lays down directions for the guidance of his converts in matters of public worship,—dealing with such questions as the wearing of a covering on the head in the public services, the duty of a modest reticence on the part of the female members of the congregation, the necessity for sobriety and decorum in the celebration of the Lord's Supper, the essential harmony and common end of the various gifts conferred by the Spirit (of which he enumerates no less than nine), the superiority of love to all such gifts, the relative value and importance of the several gifts, and the propriety of making the religious services intelligible to all, so that they may be able to join in the loud Amen as the token of their fellowship. He sums up his teaching on public worship in the two cardinal principles, "let all things be done unto edifying," "let all things be done decently and in order" (xiv. 26, 40). The 15th chapter contains a dissertation of incomparable value on the Resurrection of the dead—a doctrine which some of the Corinthians had begun to call in question, partly in a spirit of worldly-mindedness, and partly as the result of a sceptical philosophy.[1] In verses 4-8 we have a summary of evidences for the historical reality of our Lord's resurrection, stated within twenty-five or thirty years after His death, while most of the witnesses were still alive. In the 16th or closing chapter we find a number of directions and intimations having reference, among other things, to the collection for the poor saints at Jerusalem (which the apostle hoped to find ready on his next visit to Corinth),—after which the epistle concludes with the usual kind messages and autograph greeting from the apostle.

[1] It was the future general resurrection that they doubted, not the historical resurrection of Jesus Christ, the latter fact being so fully accepted that one of the apostle's chief arguments against their scepticism was that it would involve the rejection of the testimony to Christ's resurrection (xv. 13-16).

CHAPTER XI

"THE SECOND EPISTLE OF PAUL THE APOSTLE TO THE CORINTHIANS"

1. Authorship.—The Pauline authorship of this epistle is involved in that of 1 Corinthians. There is in several points such a subtle harmony between them as can only be accounted for by their common authorship; and the impression that both are genuine writings of Paul is confirmed by an examination of relative passages in the Book of Acts.[1]

That the author did not derive his information from

---

[1] The truth of this statement will be manifest to any one who will take the trouble to compare carefully the following corresponding passages with the assistance of Paley's *Horæ Paulinæ* (iv.):—

1 Cor. xvi. 5; 2 Cor. vii. 4-7; ix. 2-4 (regarding Paul's visit to Macedonia).

1 Cor. v. 1-5; 2 Cor. ii. 7, 8; vii. 7-12 (regarding the scandalous offence).

1 Cor. xvi. 1, 2; 2 Cor. viii. 10, 11; ix. 2-7 (regarding the money promised but not collected).

Acts xix. 23–xx. 1; 2 Cor. i. 3-10 (regarding the trouble which befell Paul in Asia).

2 Cor. i. 15, 16; i. 23–ii. 9; 1 Cor. xvi. 5-7; iv. 17, 18; Acts xix. 21, 22 (regarding his change of route previous to writing 1 Cor., and his motive for it).

Acts xviii. 1-5; 2 Cor. i. 19; xi. 9 (regarding Silas' and Timothy's coming to him from Macedonia).

Acts xx. 6, 7; 2 Cor. ii. 12, 13 (regarding the door opened to him at Troas).

2 Cor. x. 14-16; Acts xviii. 1-18 (regarding the limits of his missionary travels).

the Book of Acts may be inferred from the circumstance that the name of Titus, which is prominent in the epistle, is not once mentioned in Acts. The same conclusion may be drawn from a comparison of their respective allusions to the attempts made upon Paul's life and liberty at Damascus after his conversion (xi. 32; Acts ix. 23-25), as well as from the fact that the enumeration of his trials in xi. 24, 25 contains a number of striking statements which have nothing corresponding to them in the Book of Acts, though at the same time there is nothing inconsistent with them. With regard to the apparent discrepancy as to the number of his visits to Corinth (xiii. 1) see page 82.

Apart from the minute correspondences above referred to, there is a living interest and an air of reality about the epistle, scarcely ever met with in forgeries, especially of that early period.

With regard to external evidence a few echoes of expressions occurring in the epistle are to be found in the fragmentary writings that have come down to us from the beginning of the second century. By the end of that century the quotations from the epistle in the writings of Irenæus, Tertullian, etc., are explicit and unmistakable.

The amanuensis in this case was probably Timothy, as he is associated with the apostle in the opening verse.

2. The Readers.—"Unto the church of God which is at Corinth, with all the saints which are in the whole of Achaia." See page 73.

3. Date and Place of Composition.—It was evidently written a few months after the first epistle, say in the summer of 57 A.D., from some town in Macedonia, probably Thessalonica.[1]

---

[1] "From Philippi" according to note at end of epistle in A.V. But this is not so probable in view of the fact that the apostle seems

In the interval the apostle had left Ephesus (i. 8-10), after his narrow escape from the violence of the crowd, and had proceeded to Troas, where he anxiously expected the arrival of Titus. The latter had been sent to Corinth, either with the first epistle or shortly after its dispatch, to enforce the apostle's views and to bring him back word of the effect produced by his epistle at this momentous crisis in the history of his most influential Church (viii. 6; xii. 18; 1 Cor. xvi. 12).

In his disappointment at not finding Titus, he had no heart to embrace the opportunity of preaching at Troas, and had proceeded to Macedonia (ii. 12, 13), where Titus at length joined him (vii. 5, 6). It was after getting Titus' report, bringing him great relief of mind in the midst of his severe trials and heavy responsibilities (vii. 4-16; xi. 28), that he appears to have written this epistle, which he sent by the hands of Titus, accompanied by two other brethren, whom he describes as "the messengers of the churches, the glory of Christ," one of them being "the brother whose praise in the gospel is spread through all the churches," and the other "our brother, whom we have many times proved earnest in many things" (viii. 6, 16-23).[1]

A difficulty has been raised about the expression in xiii. 1, "This is the third time I am coming to you." Some think the apostle had paid a second visit to Corinth, from Ephesus, prior to the writing of his first epistle. But another explanation is to be found in the importance attaching to the visit he had intended to pay on his way to Macedonia (i. 15). The confidence of the Corinthians in him had been shaken by the disappointment he had

to have already visited the Churches of Macedonia (viii. 1-4), for in the course of doing so Philippi would naturally come first, to one travelling southward.

[1] Many attempts have been made to identify these two brethren. Luke is generally held to be one of them.

caused them; and he wished to impress upon them the
reality of his intention, although he had been unable to
fulfil it. No doubt, on this supposition, he would have
been more strictly accurate if he had expressed himself
as in xii. 14, "Behold, this is the third time I am ready
to come to you."

4. Character and Contents.—If the first epistle may
be said to be our great instructor regarding the inner life
of the Church, the second epistle is our chief source of
information regarding the personality of the apostle himself. It is an outpouring of personal feeling almost from
beginning to end, expressing itself in many different moods
and with a great variety of style. It is well described
by Erasmus when he says that "at one time the apostle
wells up gently like some limpid spring, and by and
by thunders down like a torrent with a mighty crash,
carrying everything before it; now he flows placidly and
smoothly, now spreads out far and wide, as if expanding
into a lake, then disappears, and suddenly reappears in a
different place." But although the least systematic of
Paul's writings, it contains many passages of priceless
worth, for the comfort and edification of the Church.

The apostle had learned from Titus that his first letter
had served its purpose and that the interests of Church
discipline had been secured. But the same messenger
had informed him that fresh cause for anxiety had arisen
in the rapid growth of a party hostile to his influence,
who were seeking to trade upon the disaffection which
had been caused among his converts by his failure to
visit them according to promise (i. 16, 17).

Traces of such opposition are discernible even in the
first epistle (1 Cor. i. 12; ix. 1-6); but it had been
greatly stimulated by the intrigues and false pretensions
of rival teachers from Jerusalem, who had brought letters
of commendation with them, and were using Peter's

name, and even that of Christ, for party purposes (ii. 17 ;
iii. 1, 2 ; v. 12 ; x. 7-12, 18 ; xi. 3-5, 12-15, 22, 23).

To defeat the efforts of these Judaising teachers and
to refute the charges and insinuations which they were
bringing against him was the main object of this epistle.
By doing so the apostle hoped to obviate the necessity
for any sharp dealing after he arrived at Corinth (xii.
20, 21 ; xiii. 10).

In i.-vii. Paul seeks to conciliate the affection of his
converts by giving them an account of his sufferings and
of the anxiety he had felt on their behalf. He explains
that his delay in visiting them had not been owing to
any fickleness of purpose on his part, but to a desire for
the restoration of peace and purity before he came
among them. He gives a frank exposition of his views
and feelings, his trials and supports, as a minister of
Christ, making glad and thankful acknowledgment of
the kind reception they had given to his deputy, and of
the full amends they had made in the important case of
Church discipline about which he had written to them.
In viii.-ix. he exhorts them to a prompt and liberal
fulfilment of their promise to contribute for the relief of
the needy brethren at Jerusalem,—a promise of which he
had boasted to the churches at Macedonia in order to
stimulate their generosity. In this connection he sets
forth more fully than anywhere else in his writings the
motives and dispositions which should actuate Christians
in the discharge of this duty of pecuniary liberality.

At this point there is a sudden change in the apostle's
tone ; and the remainder of the epistle (x.-xiii.) is devoted
to a vindication of his character as an apostle. He
enumerates his many claims to the respect and obedience
of his converts, and closes with an impressive salutation,
followed by the form of Benediction which has now
become so general in the Church : "The grace of the

Lord Jesus Christ, and the love of God, and the communion of the Holy Ghost, be with you all."

That the epistle succeeded in regaining, or rather in retaining, for the apostle the general confidence of his Corinthian converts, may be inferred from the veneration in which his memory was held amongst them a few years after his death. Of this veneration we find unmistakable tokens in the epistle of Clement to the Corinthians, written towards the close of the first century.

CHAPTER XII

1. Authorship.—This is another epistle whose genuineness is scarcely disputed. Its main topic—the relation of Christians to the ceremonial law of the Jews—would lead us to fix its composition at a period anterior to the destruction of Jerusalem, when the question was practically set at rest.

Its character and style are inconsistent with the idea of forgery. (1) The picture which it gives of the state of the Galatian Church is too lifelike, and the play of feeling it exhibits on the part of the apostle is too subtle for the inventive power of an age so little skilled in that kind of fiction. (2) Its representation of facts, as regards the relations of Paul with the other apostles, is too candid to have been got up in the interests of Church unity, and on the other hand is too moderate in its tone to have been framed in the interests of any known party in the Church. (3) A comparison of the personal and historical allusions in the epistle with statements in the Book of Acts and some of the other epistles ascribed to Paul, shows a substantial harmony, along with an occasional diversity that betokens independence—the epistle furnishing details of many incidents in Paul's life that are only mentioned in a general way by the author of the Book of Acts.[1] (4) There is in several respects a strong resemblance between this epistle and those to the Corinthians and the Romans (see p. 96).

With regard to external evidence there are the usual echoes and reflections in the Apostolic Fathers and in the apologists and other theological writers of the second century; while many direct quotations are to be found in the writings of the Fathers about the end of the second century. The epistle is also included in the Canons and Versions of the second century.

2. The Readers.—"Unto the churches of Galatia." The interpretation of the term "Galatia" has been a subject of much controversy. It may either be understood to refer to the recently created Roman province of that name in Asia Minor, or be taken in the older and more popular sense, as designating a broad strip of country in that province, about two hundred miles long, running from south-west to north-east.

It is in the latter sense that the term has generally been understood here. The region thus designated was inhabited by a mixed race of Phrygians, Greeks, Celts, Romans, and Jews, who had successively obtained a footing in it by different means and with varying degrees of success. Of these elements of the population it was the Celtic invaders from Western Europe that had made their influence most strongly felt. They found their way into the country in the third century B.C.; and after

---

[1] For proofs of independence, cf. i. 15-18, Acts ix. 19-26; ii. 1-10, Acts xv. 1-21; ii. 11-14 (which has nothing corresponding to it in Acts, although corroborated in some of its circumstances by xi. 25, 26; xiv. 26, xv. 1-24, xxi. 18-25). For fulness of detail in this epistle see ii.; i. 17-19, Acts ix. 25-28, xxii. 18; iv. 13, 14, cf. 2 Cor. xii. 7-9; vi. 1, cf. 2 Cor. ii. 6-8; vi. 11, cf. Rom. xvi. 22, 2 Thess. iii. 17. It must at the same time be admitted that there are a number of apparent discrepancies between this epistle and the Book of Acts which we are unable to explain, but they are not such as to justify any doubt as to the Pauline authorship of the epistle.

them and the Greek immigrants who were there before
them the country was called Gallo-Græcia. So deep and
lasting was their influence, that even in the end of the
fourth century A.D. Jerome was able to trace a strong
resemblance between the language of Galatia and that
spoken on the banks of the Moselle and the Rhine; and
modern travellers have been struck with the fair hair
and blue eyes that mark an affinity between the pastoral
tribes of Galatia and the peasantry of Western France.

Confirmation of the view that it was to the inhabitants of Celtic Galatia the epistle was addressed has
been found in the *enthusiasm*, as well as the *fickleness*
and *love of novelty*, which have been characteristic of the
Gauls both in Europe and Asia, and which left their
mark on the early history of the Galatian Church (i. 6;
iii. 1-3; iv. 13-16; v. 7). Traces have also been discerned in the epistle of the *superstition*, *drunkenness*,
avarice, *vanity*, *irascibility* and *strife* that sometimes
impair the charm of the Celtic character (v. 15, 21, 26;
vi. 3, 4, 6).

According to this theory Paul's preaching of the
Gospel in Galatia was due to his detention in that
country on his way to the more promising field of proconsular Asia, caused by an attack of the painful and
humiliating malady to which he was liable—supposed to
have been an aggravated form of ophthalmia (iv. 13-16,
cf. 2 Cor. xii. 7-10). This visit to Galatia, which took
place in the course of his second missionary journey,
about 51 A.D., is alluded to in the Book of Acts in the
most general terms (xvi. 6); but from some passages in
this epistle, already quoted, it would appear that his
faithful and energetic preaching of Christ crucified (iii.
1, 2) had excited great enthusiasm and affection. A
second visit to Galatia (implied in Gal. iv. 13) is
recorded in Acts xviii. 22, 23, during the apostle's third

missionary journey, about 54 A.D., when he "went
through the region of Galatia and Phrygia in order,
stablishing all the disciples." From this language it
appears that not a few congregations had been formed
in the district; but it would seem that their feelings
towards the apostle and his Gospel had in the meantime
undergone a change, and that he had, on this second
occasion, to speak to them in tones of warning (i. 9;
v. 21; iv. 16-20).

While the majority of scholars have hitherto been
agreed in giving to Galatia the narrower interpretation
that is assumed in the foregoing statement, a number of
critics [1] hold that the name is to be taken in its wider
meaning as a designation for the Roman province, which
included several other districts besides that of the
Asiatic Celts, and that the Churches to which the epistle
was addressed were no other than those of Antioch,
Iconium, Lystra, and Derbe, which were planted by
Paul in his first missionary journey, and of which we
have an account in Acts xiii., xiv., as well as in the
meagre notices above referred to, in chaps. xvi. and xviii.

The following are the chief arguments adduced in
support of this view :—

I. (1) The cities referred to (Antioch, Iconium, Lystra,
and Derbe) formed part of the Roman province of
Galatia in the time of the apostle. They were important
centres of Roman civilisation; and the Roman name
"Galatians" was certainly one to which their citizens

[1] Renan, Perrot, Sabatier, Hausrath, Weizsäcker, Pfleiderer, etc.
Recently a careful and elaborate argument in favour of this view has
been advanced by Professor W. M. Ramsay (*The Church in the
Roman Empire*, chaps. i.-vi.), who brings to the discussion of the
question a rare knowledge of the archæology and topography of Asia
Minor. According to Professor Ramsay, the prevailing misconception
as to the meaning of Galatia has been due to the fact that "during
the second century the term Galatia ceased to bear the sense which it
had to a Roman in the first century."

were entitled—indeed it was the only acceptable title by which they could be addressed in common. It was a mode of address congenial to the mind of the apostle, who followed the Roman lines of communication in his mission work, and regarded the Roman empire as the appointed field of his labours; and it is in accordance with his use of similar geographical terms in á Roman sense ("Macedonia," "Achaia," "Asia"). So "Galatia" in 1 Pet. i. 1.   (2) The enthusiastic reception accorded to him by the Galatians, to which the apostle refers in the epistle (iv. 14, 15), corresponds with the account given in the Book of Acts of the wonderful impression made at Antioch and elsewhere, but especially at Lystra where the cry was raised "the gods are come down to us in the likeness of men."   (3) The ritualistic tendencies supposed to have been due to Celtic influence find their true explanation in the Oriental character of the Phrygians and Lycaonians, which gave them a "strong natural affinity for the Hebraic type of Christianity."   (4) The language of vi. 17 : "From henceforth let no man trouble me : for I bear branded on my body the marks of Jesus," finds its explanation in the "persecutions, sufferings; what things befell me at Antioch, at Iconium, at Lystra" (2 Tim. iii. 11).   (5) The charge of inconsistency on the part of the apostle implied in v. 11 : "But I, brethren, if I still preach circumcision, why am I still persecuted ?" if occasioned, as it probably was, by his conduct in causing Timothy to be circumcised at Lystra, would be very likely to be brought against him by the Jews in that and the neighbouring cities.   (6) The repeated allusions to Barnabas (ii. 1, 9, 13, : ". . . insomuch that even Barnabas was carried away with their dissimulation ") give the impression that Barnabas was personally known to the readers, and seem more natural if addressed to the Churches in South Galatia, where Barnabas had

been a fellow-labourer with Paul. (7) The language of
Gal. iii. 28 : "There can be neither *Jew nor Greek*, there
can be neither bond nor free, there can be no male and
female : for ye all are one man in Christ Jesus," would
also be more appropriate if addressed to Churches in
which Greek culture was widely diffused, and where the
Jews had long made their influence felt, as was the case
in South Galatia. (8) If it was not to these Churches
that this epistle was addressed, they are left without
any share in the apostle's correspondence (so far as it
has been preserved to us) although they were the first-
fruits of his labours among the Gentiles, had been repeatedly visited by him, and were counted worthy of a
prominent place in the history of the Church by the
writer of the Book of Acts. If not included in "the
Churches of Galatia" there is only one passage in which the
apostle mentions them—in connection with the persecutions he had once suffered among them (2 Tim. iii. 11).

II. (1) Nowhere in the Book of Acts—neither in xvi.
6, 7, nor in xviii. 23, the only two passages in which
Galatia is mentioned in that book—is it implied that
St. Paul ever visited the cities of North Galatia. "The
region of Phrygia and Galatia" (xvi. 6, R.V. ; "the Phrygian and Galatian country," Lightfoot) ; "the region of
Galatia and Phrygia" (xviii. 23, R.V.), may be taken as a
general description of "some region" (to use the words
of Bishop Lightfoot, himself one of the ablest advocates
of the *North* Galatian theory) "which might be said to
belong either to Phrygia or Galatia, or the parts of each
contiguous to the other," or, according to Professor
Ramsay, the words may be taken in a still narrower sense
as equivalent to Phrygo-Galatia, *i.e.* the part of Phrygia
in the Roman province of Galatia. (2) Even assuming
that the apostle did visit North Galatia, there is no
evidence of his having *preached* there. It seems un-

likely that he should have set himself to the evangelisation of such a remote district—with its scattered cities and fatiguing journeys—when he was recovering from sickness,[1] and when the leading of the Spirit, so far as recorded, was conducting him to Europe. But, if he had done so, we should surely have found some information in the Book of Acts regarding his planting of Churches, considering the fulness with which his missionary work in other parts of Asia Minor during the same period is narrated, in accordance with the systematic plan of the author. (3) The honourable position assigned to "the Churches of Galatia" (1 Cor. xvi. 1) in connection with the charitable fund which the apostle was raising throughout the Church for the benefit of the poor Christians at Jerusalem—side by side with "Macedonia" and "Achaia" (cf. 2 Cor. ix. 1, 2)—shows that they were Churches of considerable importance, whose existence was not likely to be ignored in the Book of Acts, especially after they had been the recipients (as the author could scarcely fail to know) of such a memorable epistle. In this connection it is significant to find "Gaius of *Derbe*" as well as Timothy of *Lystra* (Acts xx. 4) among the deputies who accompanied Paul from Greece into Asia, on the way to Jerusalem to present the united offerings of the Gentile Church, whereas we look in vain for any representatives of North Galatia.

In the light of all these considerations it will be seen

---

[1] Professor Ramsay holds that the true explanation of the apostle's "infirmity of the flesh" (Gal. iv. 13) is that in his first missionary journey Paul was prostrated with a malarious fever at Perga, where he not improbably arrived during the hot season, possibly in June. Such an illness is a common experience of travellers at the present day ; and a remedy is frequently sought in such a change to the hills as that which Paul obtained when he came to Antioch (Acts xiii. 13, 14). Hitherto his face had been turned westward (Perga being on the way to Rome), and it was owing to the change of plan involved in the journey to Antioch that John Mark, who had come with Paul and Barnabas as far as Perga, returned to Jerusalem.

that the balance of probability is in favour of the South
Galatian theory—the very existence of Churches in
North Galatia, in the time of the Apostle Paul, being a
matter of conjecture.

The only other intercourse between Paul and the
Galatian Churches (besides the visits already mentioned)
of which we have any record in the New Testament is
the injunction above referred to concerning the collection
for the poor of the Church at Jerusalem. This communication may have taken place during the apostle's last
visit to these Churches, or in the course of his subsequent
stay at Ephesus, when the news may have reached him
of his converts' lapse from the truth.

Their falling away had evidently been connected with
an attempt on the part of Judaising teachers to persuade
to an observance of the ceremonial law of Moses (iii. 1-3;
iv. 10, 11, 21; v. 2-4, 7, 12; vi. 12, 13).[1] Although
the Galatian Christians were mainly converts from
heathenism (iv. 8; v. 2; vi. 12), some of them had
doubtless been connected with the Jewish synagogues,
either as members or as proselytes. Josephus tells us
that two thousand Jewish families had been settled in
Lydia and Phrygia by Antiochus the Great. Numerous
Jews had also been attracted to the cities of Galatia proper
by the commercial advantages which these afforded; and
of their privileges, Josephus tells us, a monumental record
existed in the temple of Augustus at Ancyra, the ancient
capital of the district. The existence of this Jewish
element in the Church explains the frequent allusions to
the Old Testament and the influence gained over the
Galatians by the Judaising Christians of Jerusalem, who

[1] According to the North Galatian theory, these teachers were
taking advantage of the ritualistic tendencies which, as Cæsar tells us,
were characteristic of the Gauls, and which had been fostered by the
worship of the Phrygian Cybele, with its "wild ceremonial and
hideous mutilations."

were "zealous of the law," and desired to make the Gospel tributary to the synagogue and the temple (i. 7). They had taken advantage of Paul's absence to undermine his character as an apostle, and had endeavoured only too successfully to cause a reaction, in the minds of the Galatians, from the simplicity and spirituality of the Gospel. It was an attempt to recover the ground which they had lost at Antioch and elsewhere (ii. 4, 5, 11, 14; Acts xv. 1, 23-29).

3. Date and Place of Composition.—From what has been already said as to the allusions in this epistle to the apostle's second visit to Galatia, we may infer that its composition was subsequent to 54 A.D., if we take Galatia in the narrower sense, or to 51 A.D., if we understand it to mean the Roman province of that name, which included the cities of Asia Minor visited by Paul in his first missionary journey. The expression "so soon," or rather "so quickly" (R.V.), has been thought to imply that the epistle must have been written very shortly after the second visit. But if there is any reference here to a previous event, it was probably their *calling*, or conversion, that the apostle had in view; and the language would be equally appropriate whether an interval of five or of ten years had elapsed. The expression may be better taken, however, as referring simply to the rapidity with which they succumbed to the influence of false teachers.

Another note of time has been found in the apostle's allusions to his two visits to Jerusalem (i. 18, ii. 1). Professor Ramsay [1] holds that the visits referred to could have had no bearing on the question of Paul's independent authority as an apostle to the Galatians unless they had taken place before his first appearance among them as

---

[1] *The Church in the Roman Empire*, third edition, p. 107. Cf. his instructive article in *The Expositor* for August 1895.

a preacher of the Gospel. He points out that if the Galatians were converted by the apostle during his first missionary journey, about 48 A.D.—when he preached in South Galatia — there is no discrepancy between the epistle and the Book of Acts, each telling of two visits to Jerusalem, and two only, before that period. This theory would seem to require a very early date for the apostle's conversion ("after the space of fourteen years I went up again to Jerusalem," ii. 1), but it would leave the date *of the epistle* to be further determined. If we follow the traditional view and identify the second visit referred to in the epistle with the third one recorded in the Book of Acts (chap. xv.—about 50 A.D.) in connection with the Council of Jerusalem, and suppose the difference with Peter at Antioch (ii. 11-21) to have taken place soon afterwards, the epistle may still have been written as early as 51 A.D. This or the following year is the date which some would assign to it.[1] But in all prob-

---

[1] The Rev. F. Rendall, in an able argument in *The Expositor*, vol. ix. p. 254 (1894), maintains that the epistle was written from Corinth in 52 A.D., when Paul was contending single-handed against his Jewish adversaries; and in vi. 17 he finds an allusion to the stripes recently inflicted on the apostle at Philippi, as well as to the persecutions he had suffered at Lystra. He lays stress on the absence of any direct reference in the epistle to the great scheme of Christian liberality on behalf of "the saints" at Jerusalem in which the apostle was so deeply interested in 56-58 A.D., and holds such silence to be unaccountable in an epistle written during that period. But according to Bishop Lightfoot we *have* a reference to this matter in vi. 9, 10—the warning with which it is accompanied in verses 7, 8 being due to the unsatisfactory response that had hitherto been made by the Galatians. More probably their contributions had already been secured (1 Cor. xvi. 1), and, if so, there may have been no occasion for further mention of the subject, any more than in writing to the Romans, as the apostle did shortly afterwards, or to the Philippians, Colossians, and Ephesians at a later date. More unaccountable than the apostle's silence on this matter would be the entire absence from the Epistles to the Thessalonians (written the year after the date Mr. Rendall assigns to this epistle) of any reference to the great controversy as to the relation of Law and Gospel in the Christian Church which was then, according to this theory, occupying the mind of the apostle. This

ability a considerable interval must have elapsed between the meeting of the Council at Jerusalem (whose peaceable decrees were taken to Antioch by the hands of Barsabbas and Silas, accompanying Paul and Barnabas) and the arrival at Antioch of Peter, and, subsequently, of certain men who "came from James" and induced Peter to withdraw from the fellowship of the Gentile Christians. This incident, which seems to have provoked the violent resentment of the Judaisers, probably occurred during Paul's visit to Antioch about 54 A.D., mentioned in a later chapter (Acts xviii. 22, 23), and if so, the epistle may have been written in the course of the apostle's third missionary journey, on which he entered soon afterwards. The general opinion has been that it was thus sent from Ephesus during the apostle's long residence in that city. But there seems to be good reason to assign it to a still later date, somewhere between 2 Corinthians and Romans, as we are now doing. For when we compare it with the epistles just mentioned, we find a strong resemblance to both of these—to the former in the writer's tone of feeling regarding his apostleship and the attacks made upon him; to the latter, in language, reasoning, and general cast of doctrine.[1] It was manifestly written previous to Romans, being to it as "the rough model to the finished

---

objection is only met in part by those who, like Professor Ramsay, would assign the epistle to 55 A.D., a year or two before 1 Corinthians was written, which seems to be the earliest of the series—Corinthians (Galatians), Romans—dealing with this great problem in the apostle's ministry.

[1] See Lightfoot on *Galatians*, pp. 45-49. Professor Jacobus, in the *Presbyterian and Reformed Review*, January 1895, points out that in Gal. ii. 6 we have a very near approach to the use of the composite Greek word translated "respect of persons" which Paul employs *for the first time* in Rom. ii. 11—a much nearer approach than we find in 2 Corinthians, although in the latter epistle there is a passage (x. 7) where it might have been fitly used if it had already formed part of the apostle's vocabulary even in the unconsolidated form in which it appears in Gal. ii. 6.

statue"; and it appears also to have been written when
the tension of the apostle's feelings was less severe than
when he wrote 2 Corinthians. With great probability,
therefore, we may place its composition in the period of
transition between these two epistles, towards the close
of the year 57 A.D. It may have been written in the
apostle's journey from Macedonia to Greece (Acts xx. 2),
for the expression "all the brethren which are with me"
(i. 2), in the opening salutation, would be more likely
to be used by the apostle while he was the centre of a
travelling party, than if he had been residing at the seat
of a congregation.

4. Character and Contents.—From first to last the
epistle is marked by a conspicuous unity of purpose—
its main object being to counteract the Judaising process
that had been going on for some time in the Galatian
Church. An important factor in that process had been
the denial of Paul's apostolic authority on the ground
that he had never seen the Lord, and that he owed his
knowledge of the Gospel to the apostles who had their
headquarters at Jerusalem. On the question of circumcision and the observance of the law it was alleged that
he was particularly to be distrusted, as a renegade from
the religion of his fathers.

Without a word of his usual praise and thanksgiving,
the apostle begins with a bold assertion of his apostolic
office as directly conferred upon him by the Lord. This
is followed by an account of his intercourse and relations
with the other apostles after his conversion, showing
that he owed his conception of the Gospel not to them,
but to influence exerted on him from above (*e.g.* in the
solitudes of Arabia, i. 17). His ministry had been acknowledged by the reputed pillars of the Church (James and
Cephas and John) as having the same Divine sanction
for the Gentiles, as their preaching had for the Jews.

7

Since that time he had consistently maintained the freedom of his converts from the bondage of the Law, having even gone so far on one occasion as to rebuke Peter for his dissimulation, when he would have withdrawn from fellowship with the Gentile Christians at Antioch (i. 18–ii.).

Having thus disposed of the personal aspect of the question, he passes to its more doctrinal aspect by appealing to the spiritual blessing which the Galatians had experienced under his ministry when he preached the Gospel to them without any mixture of Jewish ritual. He proves that the Law has been superseded by the Gospel, the latter being the full assertion of that principle of faith that had always lain at the foundation of men's acceptance with God, even in the time of Abraham. He shows that the Law given by Moses could only create a sense of sin without providing a remedy. It was but a temporary means of training God's people for the enjoyment of their privileges as His children—standing in the same relation to the Gospel, as the children of Hagar the bondwoman did to Isaac the child of promise (iii.-iv.). In v.-vi. the apostle warns them against the abuse of their spiritual freedom, setting before them the true principles of Christian morality, and exhorting them to several duties of which they had need to be reminded. He concludes with a postscript in his own handwriting (vi. 11-18), in which he sums up the argument with an emphasis and decision that contrast strongly with the hesitation apparent in some of the earlier passages, where he is trying to vindicate his conduct without casting any unnecessary reflections on the other apostles. He exposes the unworthy motives of his opponents, reaffirms the supreme importance of the Cross of Christ[1] and of regeneration in Him as essential to the true Israel of

[1] The name of Christ occurs forty-three times in this short epistle.

God, and appeals to the marks which he bears of recent persecution, as the seal of his apostleship and the token of his renewed devotion to the Saviour. "From henceforth let no man trouble me, for I bear branded on my body the marks of Jesus."[1] Finally he invokes the Divine blessing on his converts in terms specially fitted to lift them above the thought of carnal ordinances—"The grace of our Lord Jesus Christ be -with your spirit, brethren."

The whole epistle is marked by a force and vehemence that strain the apostle's power of expression to the utmost. It has done more than any other book of the New Testament for the emancipation of Christians, not only from the yoke of Judaism, but from every other form of externalism that has ever threatened the freedom and spirituality of the Gospel.[2] It was Luther's favourite epistle, to which he was "wedded," as he said ; and from it he largely drew his inspiration in his conflict with the Church of Rome.

[1] With this we may connect the fact that in the very next epistle which he writes Paul styles himself "a bondservant of Jesus Christ" (Rom. i. 1, R.V. margin), being the first time, so far as is known, that he ever so designated himself.

[2] The words "free," "freedom," "make free," occur eleven times in the epistle.

CHAPTER XIII

1. Authorship.—The Pauline authorship of this epistle is universally admitted. There is no lack of external evidence in its favour; but its strong resemblance to Galatians is enough to prove its common authorship with that epistle. Moreover, a comparison of its contents with other Pauline epistles and with the Book of Acts affords valuable confirmation of its genuineness and authenticity.[1]

From one of the closing salutations (xvi. 22) we learn

---

[1] Besides the remarkable coincidences with regard to the time and place of its composition, p. 102, the following points are worthy of notice. (1) The statement of the writer's long-felt desire to visit Rome, and of his hope of now doing so after fulfilling his mission to Jerusalem, is in harmony with the purpose expressed by the apostle at Ephesus some time before, i. 13; xv. 22-25; Acts xix. 21. (2) The request which he makes to the Christians at Rome that they would unite with him in prayer that he "may be delivered from them that are disobedient in Judæa," corresponds with the apostle's expression of feeling in his last journey to Jerusalem (xv. 30, 31; Acts xx. 22, 23). (3) The teaching in this epistle and in Galatians is in striking harmony with Paul's mission as the apostle of the Gentiles, and goes far to explain the accusation brought against him on his last recorded visit to Jerusalem (Acts xxi. 19). (4) The nature of the visit to Rome contemplated by the writer of this epistle, namely, "that I may come unto you in joy through the will of God, and together with you find rest" (xv. 32), is so very different from what the apostle actually experienced, when he was carried a prisoner to Rome, that it could not have been so described by any one who derived his information from the Book of Acts.

that the epistle was written by Tertius as the apostle's amanuensis.

2. The Readers.—"To all that are in Rome, beloved of God, called to be saints." These words and the absence of any mention of bishops and deacons either in this epistle or in the account of the welcome which Paul received from the Roman brethren three years afterwards (Acts xxviii. 15) would seem to indicate that there was no formally organised Church in the city, but merely groups of believers meeting for worship in private houses (xvi. 5). They seem to have been mainly of Gentile origin (i. 5, 6, 13-15; xi. 13-24; xv. 15, 16). But the whole tenor of the epistle, abounding as it does in quotations from the Old Testament (more than sixty in number) and in allusions to the Jewish Law, clearly shows that they had been led to a knowledge of the truth through their connection with the Jewish faith as proselytes of the gate (indeed, some of them appear to have been born Jews—ii. 17; xvi. 7—and hence the expression, "I speak to men that know the law," vii. 1). The Jews had for a long time been a numerous and powerful section of the community at Rome, and their religion had gained great influence among the educated classes.[1] The introduction of Christianity among them had apparently been due not to apostolic labours (certainly not to those of Peter,[2] whose alleged episcopate of twenty-five

---

[1] Thousands of Jewish captives were brought to Rome by Pompey from the East, about 63 B.C.; and from that time forward the Jews continued to grow in numbers and influence until, in the next century, Seneca could say of them, Victoribus victi leges dederunt, "The conquered have given laws to their conquerors."

[2] "It is not without significance that, among the frescoes of the Catacombs, the only figure of an apostle which is represented separately from the rest of the twelve is that of St. Paul, described as PAULUS PASTOR APOSTOLUS, side by side with a figure of the Good Shepherd. In none of the Catacombs is St. Peter specially designated by name or attribute."—Marriott's *Testimony of the Catacombs*.

years at Rome is unsupported by evidence in the New
Testament or elsewhere), but to the influence of Christian travellers, especially, we may believe, of the "sojourners from Rome, both Jews and proselytes," who had
witnessed the wonderful works of God on the great day
of Pentecost (Acts ii. 10). Although Paul had never
been at Rome, many of the Christians there were personally known to him—possibly owing to their temporary
banishment from Rome by the Edict of Claudius,—as
we may infer from the numerous greetings in the closing
chapter. From i. 7, 8; xv. 14, it would appear that the
religious condition of the Christians at Rome was in many
respects satisfactory ; and in keeping with this we learn
from Tacitus that a great multitude of them endured
martyrdom in the reign of Nero a few years later. But
the apostle's language (in chap. xiv.) would indicate the
existence of weakness and disagreement among them,
in connection with certain scruples felt by some of their
number with regard to the eating of animal food and the
observance of days and seasons. They were also liable
to many serious temptations, as we may infer from the
exhortations in xii.-xiii. ; and their spiritual life required
to be strengthened (i. 11).

3. **Date and Place of Composition.**—From the writer's
circumstances, as. stated in xv. 22-26, viewed in the
light of Acts xx. 1-3, xxiv. 17-19 ; 1 Cor. xvi. 1-4 ; 2 Cor.
viii. 1-4, ix. 1, 2, we gather that the epistle was written
towards the close of Paul's second visit to Corinth (early
in 58 A.D.), on the eve of his journey to Jerusalem to
carry up the alms collected for the poor brethren there,
after which he was to make his long-intended visit to
Rome.[1]

[1] In remarkable harmony with this inference as to the *date* of the
epistle are the facts (1) that of those who "accompanied Paul as far
as Asia" (Acts xx. 4) on his last journey towards Jerusalem, three,
namely, Sosipater, Gaius, and Timothy, send their salutations in this

4. Character and Contents.—In an intellectual sense this epistle may be said to be the apostle's masterpiece; theologically it is the most important of all his epistles. Coleridge has pronounced it "the most profound work ever written." Calvin said of it that "it opened the door to all the treasures in the Scriptures"; while Luther considered it "the chief book of the New Testament, and the purest Gospel."

As already mentioned, it bears a striking resemblance to Galatians (written a short time before it) not only in individual words and phrases, but in the general drift of its teaching with regard to the superiority of the Gospel to the Law. It is, however, more dispassionate in tone, being less personal in its character, and containing a more full and comprehensive treatment of the subject.

It may be said to embody the results of the recent controversy with the Judaisers, stated in a logical and

epistle; (2) that salutations are sent to Priscilla and Aquila (xvi. 3), who are mentioned as having rendered great service and incurred great danger on behalf of the apostle and in the interests of the Church of the Gentiles—which finds confirmation in Acts xviii. 2-26; 1 Cor. xvi. 19; (3) that the apostle speaks (xv. 19) of having preached the Gospel "from Jerusalem, and round about even unto Illyricum" —a country adjoining the western frontier of Macedonia,—a statement which could not have been made before his second recorded visit to Europe (Acts xx. 1, 2), as on the first occasion his visit was confined to the towns along its eastern coast (Acts xvi.-xviii.).

Equally in keeping with the inference as to the *place* of composition, viz. Corinth, are the facts (1) that "Gaius my host" and "Erastus the treasurer of the city" send their greetings (xvi. 23), the former being mentioned in 1 Cor. i. 14 as one of the very few persons at Corinth whom the apostle had himself baptized, the latter in Acts xix. 22 as a companion of Paul and in 2 Tim. iv. 20 as left behind at Corinth; (2) that Phœbe, by whom the epistle was apparently conveyed to Rome, is commended (xvi. 1, 2) as "a servant of the church that is at Cenchreæ," which was one of the ports of Corinth that had been previously visited by Paul (Acts xviii. 18).

In connection with the mention of Phœbe it is interesting to observe that even at this early period the Christian Church had learned to appreciate the value of female energy and devotion.

systematic form, and at the same time with such moderation and caution as was fitted to disarm the prejudices
and conciliate the favour of the·Jewish element in the
Church.   That element had not yet been infected with
the leaven of malignant bigotry, emanating from Jerusalem, which had made its influence felt in so many of
the other Churches where Paul had laboured ; and the
epistle was intended to serve the purpose of prevention
rather than cure.   It was also intended to pave the way
for the apostle's visit to the Church at Rome, whose
destined greatness he foresaw, and by whose assistance
he hoped to obtain a still wider field for his missionary
labours.[1]

Being addressed to the Christians of imperial Rome,
this epistle is distinguished by its cosmopolitan tone,
which is shown at the outset (i. 4, 5) by a reference to
the "obedience of faith" to which "all the nations" are
called in "Jesus Christ our Lord."   It sets forth the
universality of the Gospel as "the power of God unto salvation to every one that believeth ; to the Jew first, and
also to the Greek"[2] (i. 16), and brings out the contrast
not between Moses and Christ, as in Galatians, but
between Adam and Christ as the representatives of
nature and of grace (v. 12-21).   With no less propriety,
in writing to the inhabitants of a city that was the seat
of justice for the whole civilised world, the apostle looks
at the great question of salvation from a judicial or
forensic point of view, — exhibiting the bearing of the

---

[1] "In time of war, a good general knows well the importance of
seizing commanding positions, and discerns them by a sort of intuition.
St. Paul had this faculty, as a leader of that little army which, with
its spiritual weapons of warfare, went forth to subdue the nations to
Christ : and, while journeying in the east, he kept this steadily in
view : 'I must also see Rome'" (Fraser's *Synoptical Lectures*, Third
Series, p. 13).

[2] The word "all" or "every" occurs nearly seventy times in the
epistle.

Gospel on the interests of law and righteousness, proving
the guilt of all men, both Jews and Gentiles, at the bar
of Divine judgment, and proclaiming the doctrine of
justification by faith as the only means of acceptance
with God.

Having set forth the great scheme of redemption, the
apostle deals with its bearing on the fortunes of the
chosen people (ix.-xi.). He shows that their failure to
enter into the blessings of the New Covenant, which
gave him "great sorrow and unceasing pain in (his)
heart," was due to their own spiritual blindness, as fore-
told in the writings of the prophets. Their recent experience was in keeping with the analogy of God's dealings
with them in the past, but their rejection was only
partial and temporary, destined to lead in the mysterious
wisdom of Divine providence to a still fuller manifestation
of Divine goodness. "For God hath shut up all unto dis-
obedience, that he might have mercy upon all" (xi. 32).

After this lesson on the philosophy of history, in which
the apostle seeks to justify the ways of God to men and
is moved again and again to adoration of the Divine
wisdom, he exhorts his readers to the cultivation of
various graces and virtues as the best refutation of the
charge of lawlessness to which the gospel of the free
grace of God is liable (xii.-xiv.). In conclusion, he sends
numerous greetings to individual Christians with whom
he is personally acquainted, many of whom had rendered
valuable service to the Church, and with whom he had
probably been brought into contact at Ephesus and other
great centres.

There are several breaks in the epistle where it might
have fitly terminated. This circumstance, together with
variations in the arrangement of the last two chapters in
some of the MSS. (and the blanks left in a MS. of some
importance where the words " in Rome " occur in the

opening chapter, vv. 7 and 14), has given rise to the idea
that the epistle was sent as an encyclical or circular-
letter, with varying terminations, to a number of Churches.
We may add that the fact of this epistle, although
addressed to Romans, being written in Greek, is not only
in keeping with the apostle's literary habit, but is also in
accordance with the general use of Greek at the time
throughout the civilised world.   The Christian congregations of the first century were like so many Greek colonies,
as far as language was concerned ; and it was not till the
latter part of the second century that a Latin version
and a Latin literature arose, chiefly for the benefit of the
Christians in North Africa.[1]   It may be noted that most
of those to whom the apostle sends salutations in this
epistle bear Greek names.

---

[1] " Even later, the ill-spelt, ill-written inscriptions of the catacombs,
with their strange intermingling of Greek and Latin characters, show
that the Church (in Rome) was not yet fully nationalised " (Lightfoot).

CHAPTER XIV

AFTER the letter to the Romans there is an interval of three or four years before we can trace any further correspondence on the part of the apostle. Leaving Corinth in the spring of 58 A.D., he made his way to Jerusalem along the coast of Macedonia and Asia Minor. In the course of his journey we find him taking farewell of one Church after another, under a strong presentiment of approaching calamity. Soon after his arrival in Jerusalem, he was arrested on account of a tumult resulting from a last effort which he made to conciliate the Jewish Christians. Removed as a prisoner to Cæsarea, he was there detained in custody for two years under the governor Felix; but, soon after the appointment of Festus as the successor of Felix, the apostle appealed for trial to the imperial judgment-seat, and was sent to Rome accordingly, under a military escort. After a disastrous voyage, in which he suffered shipwreck on the island of Malta, where he had to pass the winter, he arrived at Rome in the early summer of 61 A.D.—his long-cherished wish at length realised, but in a very different manner from what he had at one time anticipated. Owing to protracted delay in the hearing of his case—a thing by no means uncommon under the

Emperors—he remained for two years in military custody, his right hand chained to the left hand of the soldier who guarded him. He was permitted, however, to reside in his own hired lodging, and to hold free converse with friends and visitors.

It was during this period that the epistles to the *Philippians*, the *Colossians*, *Philemon*, and the *Ephesians* were composed. Each of these epistles bears tokens of having been written during the author's imprisonment (Phil. i. 7, 13, 14, 17; Col. iv. 3, 18; Philemon vv. 9, 10, 13; Eph. iii. 1, iv. 1; cf. Acts xxviii. 16, 20). It is further evident that this imprisonment was occasioned by his preaching of the Gospel to the Gentiles (Col. i. 24-27; Eph. vi. 19, 20; Acts xxii. 21, 22, xxvi. 19-21). Some think that the imprisonment in question was that which the apostle endured at Cæsarea. But in several respects the circumstances referred to in the epistles harmonise better with his stay in Rome. (*a*) The impression made by his bonds which "became manifest in Christ throughout the whole prætorian guard, and to all the rest" (Phil. i. 13), and the mention of "Cæsar's household" (iv. 22), point to the imperial city as the scene of his influence.[1] (*b*) The apostle's purpose of visiting Macedonia after his release (ii. 24), would not answer to his state of mind while he was looking forward to a visit to Rome. (*c*) The expression used in Acts xxviii. 20 to describe Paul's confinement, namely, "this chain," is almost identical with the language of Eph. vi. 20 (margin) on the same subject; while the same cannot be said of the apostle's allusion to his condition at Cæsarea when he replied to Agrippa, "I would to God,

[1] "The camp and the court were always centres of Christianising influence" (Mommsen). Cæsar's household formed an immense establishment, including thousands of slaves and freedmen employed in all kinds of official and domestic duties (as we learn from recently discovered monuments in Rome).

that whether with little or with much, not thou only, but also all that hear me this day, might become such as I am, except *these bonds*" (Acts xxvi. 29).   (*d*) Both Colossians and Philippians are written in the name of Paul and Timothy, but we find no trace of the latter in connection with Paul's imprisonment at Cæsarea.   (*e*) The great metropolis of the world was a much more likely refuge than Cæsarea for a runaway slave like Onesimus.

With regard to the order in which these four epistles were written, many critics have been disposed to assign Philippians to a. later date than the three others.   But none of their arguments when examined appear to have much weight.   Philemon—which can be shown to be contemporaneous with Colossians (see p. 118)—affords as probable an indication of having been written when the imprisonment was drawing to a close (ver. 23) as anything to be found in Philippians.   We cannot, however, infer much from such expressions, as the apostle's prospects may have undergone various vicissitudes during his imprisonment.   We are on safer ground when we base our judgment on the general character of the several epistles.   When we do so we are led to the conclusion that this epistle marks the transition from Romans to Colossians and Ephesians.   While the former of these resembles it in many points both verbal and doctrinal,[1] we discern in the two latter a new phase of doctrine of which scarcely any trace can be found in the Epistle to the Philippians.

While Philippians, therefore, was probably anterior in

[1] Cf. Phil. i. 3-8, Rom. i. 8-11 ; Phil. i. 10, Rom. ii. 18 ; Phil. iii. 4, 5, Rom. xii. 1 ; Phil. iii. 9, Rom. x. 3 ; Phil. iii. 10, 11, Rom. vi. 5. In a general sense the similarity of these two epistles as contrasted with Colossians and Ephesians may be accounted for by the former being addressed to Churches in *Europe*, the latter to the theosophic Christians of *Asia Minor*; but if Philippians had been written subsequently to them, it could scarcely have failed to bear very distinct traces of the speculative questions which had so recently engaged the apostle's attention.

date to the three others, the effects which the apostle's "bonds" are stated to have already produced in Rome (i. 13), as well as the account of Epaphroditus' mission from Philippi to Rome, with its attendant circumstances (ii., iv.), imply that some considerable time had elapsed since the apostle's arrival. We may therefore assign this epistle to the early part of 62 A.D., and the three others to the close of the same year or the beginning of 63 A.D.[1]

"THE EPISTLE OF PAUL THE APOSTLE TO THE PHILIPPIANS"

1. Authorship.—The Pauline authorship of this epistle is generally admitted. It is a characteristic outpouring of the apostle's tender, affectionate, and devout heart; the circumstances which gave rise to it come out in the course of the epistle in a casual and unaffected manner; and corroboration of them is found in the Book of Acts and elsewhere. It is difficult to imagine what purpose a forger could have had, or how he could ever have achieved success, in fabricating a letter of such a distinctly personal character.

With regard to external evidence, traces of expressions used in the epistle may be found in many of the earliest Christian writers (outside of the New Testament) whose works have come down to us. By the close of the second century its general acceptance in the Church is beyond the possibility of doubt. One writer (Tertullian, about

---

[1] It is possible the apostle may have written other letters during his imprisonment. His anxiety about his own prospects did not prevent him from engaging in active labour among the soldiers and others brought into contact with him, or from superintending by means of his colleagues and envoys the various Churches which looked to him for guidance. In this connection the following names occur in the epistles—Luke, Timothy, John Mark, Demas, Jesus Justus, Epaphroditus (of Philippi), Tychicus (of Ephesus), Epaphras (of Colossæ), and Aristarchus (of Thessalonica).

200 A.D.) states that it had all along been read and acknowledged by the Church of Philippi.

2. The Readers.—"To all the saints in Christ Jesus which are at Philippi, with the bishops and deacons." Philippi was the first place at which St. Paul preached the Gospel in Europe—in the course of his second missionary journey, 52 A.D. A very full and graphic account of this visit is given by St. Luke, who along with Timothy and Silas accompanied the apostle on the occasion (Acts xvi. 11-40). The city lay a few miles inland from the coast of Macedonia, at the confluence of Asiatic and European life on the great Egnatian highway, where there was a pass in the mountain barrier stretching north and south. Founded on an ancient site by Philip, king of Macedonia (who named it after himself) in the middle of the fourth century B.C., the city was raised to the dignity of a Roman colony by Augustus (42 A.D.) in commemoration of his great victory over Brutus and Cassius gained in the immediate vicinity. As a colony it became politically "a miniature likeness of Rome"; and the high sense of Roman citizenship which pervaded the community may be seen at several points in Luke's narrative (Acts xvi. 20, 21, 35-39) as well as in allusions in the epistle (i. 27, R.V. margin; iii. 20, R.V.). There were comparatively few Jews in the place, as we may infer from the want of any regular synagogue and the absence of any Hebrew name in the list of converts.[1] Only three members of the Church are specially mentioned in the account of Paul's visit. These are a proselyte of Asia, a Greek, and a Roman—representing the catholic nature of the Church which Paul had come to establish,—representing, too, the liberal and liberating spirit of the Gospel, two of them being women, and one

---

[1] To this fact the constant loyalty of the Philippians to the person and teaching of the apostle was probably in some measure due.

of the two a slave, the absolute property of her master.
The consecrating influence of the Gospel on family
relations is brought out here for the first time in the
history of the Church, — Lydia's "household" being
baptized with her, and the jailor rejoicing greatly "with
all his house." The prominence assigned to women both
here and in the neighbouring Churches of Thessalonica
and Berœa (Acts xvi. 13; Acts xvii. 4, 12; cf. iv. 2, 3)
is in harmony with what we know from other sources to
have been characteristic of Macedonian society.[1]

Paul's visit to Philippi was memorable not only for
the converts whom he made but also for the sufferings he
endured and the signal deliverance that was granted to
him. The Church which he then formed excelled all
others in its devoted attachment to his person and its
repeated acts of generosity to him. This generosity he
accepted, contrary to his ordinary rule, because of his
perfect confidence in the sincerity and affection of the
donors.

We hear of two subsequent visits which the apostle
paid to Philippi—in 57 and 58 A.D. (Acts xx. 2, 6). His
experience on these occasions, as well as in other com-
munications which he held with them, had done much to
cheer his heart. In their contributions for the relief of
the poor saints at Jerusalem they appear to have con-
tributed, in common with the other Macedonians, even
"beyond their power" in "much proof of affliction"
and "deep poverty" (2 Cor. viii. 1-4).

3. **Date and Place of Composition.**—At Rome, 61-62
A.D. (see pp. 108, 109).

4. **Character and Contents.**—Of all St. Paul's epistles
this is the most benign, breathing a spirit of the warmest

---

[1] "The extant Macedonian inscriptions seem to assign to the sex a
higher social influence than is common among the civilised nations of
antiquity" (Lightfoot).

sympathy and approval. At chap. iv. 1 he addresses the
Philippians as "my brethren beloved and longed for,
my joy and crown." In this respect it surpasses even
1 Thessalonians, which it resembles not a little in its
gentle and confiding tone.

Without any assertion of apostolic authority, it begins
with a very full thanksgiving for the tokens of grace
which the Philippians had so generally manifested since
the Gospel was preached among them. These tokens
led the apostle to cherish a confident persuasion that
they would advance more and more in the Christian life
and realise a fulfilment of his constant prayer on their
behalf (i. 1-11).

He then adverts to his own circumstances, and refers
to the salutary influence of his bonds in witnessing for
Christ among the imperial guard and in the city generally, while his friends were stimulated by his example,
and even his enemies were provoked to greater activity
on his account.[1] The preaching of the Gospel by these
latter, however unworthy their motives, he regards as
better than none for those who know not Christ; and
instead of troubling himself about their opposition to
him, he will rather take comfort from their labour, feeling
assured that all his trials will work together for good.
He is prepared either for life or for death, as the will of the
Lord may be, although he has a strong impression that
he will be delivered and permitted to visit Philippi once
more (i. 12-26). In any case he would appeal to them to
be firm and united in defence of Christ's cause—counting
it a token of salvation that they are permitted "not only

---

[1] These factious teachers (i. 15-17) may either have been Judaisers
(cf. iii. 1-9) or Antinomians (cf. iii. 18, 19). The latter may have
resented the apostle's warnings against their exaggeration and perver-
sion of the Gospel, and his consideration for the Jews (Rom. vi., etc.);
and they may have tried, in consequence, to slight his authority and
curtail his influence during his imprisonment.

to believe on him, but also to suffer in his behalf"
(i. 27-30).   He would counsel them to avoid all rivalry
and self-seeking, and to cultivate that humility which was
so signally displayed by the Lord Jesus Christ, and was
attended in His case with such glorious results.   He
exhorts them to work out their salvation with fear and
trembling as in God's presence and with God's help,
striving to walk worthy of their calling and to justify
the apostle's boast concerning them.   They might rest
assured that he was as devoted to their interests as ever,
and was ready, if need be, to give up his life on their
behalf.   He hoped soon to send to them their mutual and
trusty friend Timothy with news of his prospects, and
in return he hopes to hear of their state before he visits
them in person.   Meanwhile he is sending to them
Epaphroditus, the messenger of their bounty, who has
been of invaluable service to him since his arrival, but
whose recent illness and anxiety on their account render
it expedient that he should return to Philippi (ii.).

At this point (iii. 1) it would seem as if the apostle
had intended to draw to a close—probably by a renewal
of his counsels to unity and brotherly love.   But from
some cause—perhaps owing to his being interrupted by
fresh news of the Judaisers—he launches into a new
subject, warning his converts against the infatuation of
those who would put their confidence in Jewish rights or
privileges, and avowing his own renunciation of all such
claims, in view of the new life which comes from fellowship with the risen and exalted Christ.   That life cannot
be realised without strenuous and persevering effort in
the path of duty.   He would therefore caution them
against the gross abuse of the doctrines of grace which
some are guilty of, and he bids them take his own life as
an example of the Christian course.   In the last chapter
he returns to the subject of the dissensions among them,

and refers to two women of influence in the Church whom
he is anxious to see restored to terms of friendship.   For
this purpose he invokes the aid of Epaphroditus ("true
yoke-fellow ") and other leading members of the Church.
He adds several exhortations of a general nature that are
among the most beautiful precepts in the New Testament
(iv. 4-9).   In conclusion, before sending the final salutations, he thanks the Philippians warmly for the renewal
of their bounty towards him, which he welcomes not so
much on his own account as for the evidence it affords of
their devotion to the Gospel.   For their kindness to him
God will yet reward them with the higher treasures that
are hid in Christ Jesus (iv. 10-23).[1]

It is worthy of note that the "bishops and deacons"
specially addressed in the opening of the epistle (i. 1) represent the only two classes of local Church office-bearers
that are mentioned in the New Testament.   The former
(bishops or *overseers*, R.V. margin) are virtually identical
with the "elders " or presbyters mentioned elsewhere in
connection with Churches mainly composed of Jewish
converts.   To these bishops or elders were entrusted
governing and teaching functions in the Church, while the
deacons appear to have been specially charged with the
care of the poor.   The three Episcopal orders of bishop,
priest, and deacon cannot be distinctly traced before the
beginning of the second century.   -

[1] "Of the church which stood foremost among all the apostolic
communities in faith and love, it may literally be said that not one
stone stands upon another.   Its whole career is a signal monument of
the inscrutable counsels of God.   Born into the world with the
brightest promise, the church of Philippi has lived without a history
and perished without a memorial. . . . The city itself has long been a
wilderness " (Lightfoot).

CHAPTER XV

COLOSSIANS—PHILEMON

"THE EPISTLE OF PAUL THE APOSTLE TO THE COLOSSIANS"

1. Authorship.—The Pauline authorship of this epistle, as well as of that to the Ephesians (which it closely resembles), has of recent years been called in question, not for any want of external evidence, but because of its peculiar phraseology as compared with the earlier epistles of Paul. This objection, however, is one of little force. It is no uncommon thing for a writer's vocabulary to undergo a considerable change in the course of a very short period, when he is placed amid new surroundings and under the influence of new associations.[1] Anything strange about the apostle's language in this epistle is sufficiently explained by the circumstances under which he wrote, and was evidently occasioned by the new errors which he was called to encounter.

It is alleged, however, that we have in this epistle, not only novelty in language, but also in doctrine, especially with regard to the nature and office of Christ. But the truth is we have in the Christology of this epistle only the full development of ideas which had germinated in

---

[1] A close examination of the works of Xenophon, for example, has brought to light a remarkable variation of language in the books he wrote after he began to move about from place to place like St. Paul.

the apostle's mind years before (1 Thess. i. 1; 1 Cor. viii.
6, xi. 3 ; 2 Cor. iv. 4), and are to be found in other books
of the New Testament (1 John i. 3 ; Heb. i. 2).   In the
notable passage in Philippians (ii. 5-11) regarding the
original glory and the ultimate exaltation of the Saviour,
as lofty a claim is made on His behalf to the reverence
and adoration of the Church as is anywhere to be found
in this epistle.

It is worthy of note, too, that this epistle has a special
mark of genuineness in the singular connection which
subsists between it and the Epistle to Philemon (iv. 7-18,
Philemon 2, 10-12, 23, 24).[1]

2. The Readers.—"To the saints and faithful brethren in Christ which are at Colossæ."   The Church at
Colossæ seems to have been the least important of the
Churches to which Paul is known to have written.   The
city itself had at one time been populous and important,
but its prosperity was very much reduced before the days
of the apostle.   It lay on the river Lycus, a tributary of
the Mæander in the Phrygian part of Asia Minor, not
many miles distant from its more prosperous neighbours,
Laodicea and Hierapolis (iv. 13), in "a sombre and melan-
choly region" covered with the traces of volcanic action.
In common with these cities, Colossæ had doubtless been
indebted for its knowledge of Christianity to the evangel-
istic labours of Paul at Ephesus, the metropolis of the
district, from which his influence had spread far and

---

[1] This connection is such, that if the letter to Philemon be genuine
(as generally admitted), Colossians must likewise be so ; otherwise it
must be a forgery founded on Philemon.   But this is seen to be very
unlikely when it is remembered that—(1) in the Epistle to Philemon
there is no mention whatever of Colossæ, or of any place in its neighbourhood, nor yet of the messenger Tychicus ; (2) there are variations
in the salutations sent in the two epistles, such as we can scarcely
imagine to have been resorted to in the interests of forgery ; and (3)
in Colossians there is no reference whatever to Philemon himself or to
the peculiar circumstances of Onesimus as a runaway slave.

wide, "almost throughout all Asia" (Acts xix. 10, 26; 1 Cor. xvi. 19). Although we may infer from his language in the epistle (ii. 1) that Paul had not personally laboured among the Colossians, it would seem that their chief evangelist, Epaphras, had been one of his disciples (i. 7, R.V.).

This Epaphras had paid a visit to Rome during Paul's imprisonment there. Whether he had come for the express purpose of consulting the apostle regarding the state of the Colossians is not clear; but at all events he made Paul acquainted with the dangers that were besetting the Church notwithstanding many tokens of grace (i. 3-8; ii. 8-20; iv. 12, 13). The interest in Colossæ which was thus awakened in the mind of the apostle by his conversation with Epaphras was further stimulated by his intercourse with Onesimus, a runaway slave from the same city, who was in some way or other brought under his influence at Rome, and proved an invaluable friend (iv. 9, cf. Philemon). He could not permanently retain Onesimus in his service, as he was the lawful property of another, so he took the opportunity afforded by the mission of Tychicus (a trusty delegate) to Asia (iv. 7-9; Acts xx. 4; 2 Tim. iv. 12) to send Onesimus along with him, giving the latter a conciliatory letter to his master Philemon (pp. 121-125), and at the same time he addresses a longer communication to the members of the Colossian Church, with special reference to the evils to which they were exposed. This he entrusts to the care of Tychicus, by whom he also despatches another epistle intended for a still wider circle of readers (Eph. vi. 21, 22).

3. **Date and Place of Composition.**—At Rome, 62-63 A.D. (pp. 108-110).

4. **Character and Contents.**—It has been remarked that this epistle lacks the vivacity and fluency which

characterise the apostle's style when he is addressing
readers personally known to him.

To the ordinary reader it is probably the most difficult
of Paul's epistles, owing to the fact that it was designed
to be a corrective of certain errors of a recondite nature
with which we have little or nothing to do at the present
day.   For these errors the Jewish element of the population, which was so prevalent in that part of the world,
was largely responsible.[1]   It was not the Pharisees, however, whose endeavours, at an earlier period, to foist the
ceremonial law of the Jews on the Christian Church had
been so strenuously and successfully resisted by the
apostle of the Gentiles, but the Essenes, another sect of
the Jews, that were now the corrupters of the faith.
Their pretensions were of a more abstruse and philosophic
character, savouring of combined mysticism and asceticism ; and along with their teaching was mingled the
theosophy of Asia Minor, resulting in the strange form
of heresy which we find the apostle combating in this
epistle.

The heresy was partly speculative, partly practical,
but at the root of the whole there lay an abhorrence of
matter as the abode of evil, and a consequent depreciation
of everything connected with man's physical existence.
This led, on its speculative side, to an elaborate system
of mediation between the Supreme Being and the world
of matter, by means of a spiritual hierarchy consisting of
a graduated series of emanations from the deity, the

[1] Two thousand Jewish families were brought by Antiochus the
Great from Babylonia and Macedonia, and settled in Lydia and
Phrygia.   We have evidence of their numbers and wealth at a later
period in the large quantity of gold that was confiscated by the Roman
governor on its way to Jerusalem in payment of the poll-tax.   We also
find Phrygia mentioned (Acts ii. 10) as one of the countries from which
devout men were present at Jerusalem on the great day of Pentecost.
Their influence in the Colossian Church may be traced in ii. 11, 14, 16,
18, etc.

lowest of which was supposed to have been far enough removed from the Supreme Being to be capable of bringing into existence the base material world. In opposition to this theory the apostle insists upon the absolute and universal mediatorship of Christ—in the outward universe created through Him (i. 16) as well as in the Church of which He is the Head (i. 18), and warns his converts against being led astray by a false philosophy, associated with the worship of angels, which some of their teachers were trying to introduce into the Church.

On its practical side the error took the form of a rigorous asceticism, intended to free man's spirit from the degrading influence of the world and the flesh. To counteract this tendency, the apostle proclaims the inspiring and life-giving power of fellowship with Jesus Christ, by whose death upon the Cross reconciliation has been effected between heaven and earth, and in whom "dwelleth all the fulness of the Godhead bodily." The spirit of Christ ought to raise Christians above the mere elements or "rudiments" of the world, imparting to them new motives and a higher consciousness; and the apostle calls upon his readers to consecrate "in Christ" all departments of their personal and social life.

While the speculative and practical aspects of the subject are not kept entirely distinct, the former is chiefly dealt with in the first chapter, after the opening salutation, thanksgiving, and prayer; while the second chapter is more polemical in tone, and forms an introduction to the practical exhortations which occupy the third and part of the fourth or last chapter. The remainder of the epistle (iv. 7-18) is occupied with salutations and personal explanations and directions.

In several passages a reference may be traced to the intellectual pride and exclusiveness which were associated with the errors of the Colossian Church. Among its Jewish members, the pride of intellect was taking the place of the old pride of nationality. In opposition to this tendency the apostle declares that "in Christ" —not in any philosophy which man could devise— "are all the treasures of wisdom and knowledge hidden" (ii. 3). He prays that they "may be filled with the knowledge of his will in all spiritual wisdom and understanding" (i. 9). He represents the Gospel as a "mystery" that has been "manifested" to the whole Church—his duty as an apostle being to proclaim Christ, "admonishing every man, and teaching every man in all wisdom; that he may present every man perfect in Christ" (i. 25-28; ii. 2, 3). He thus declares the Church to be a spiritual democracy in which there is no room for any privileged class or inner circle of disciples,—even the Scythians, the least refined of nations, being raised to the same level, in a spiritual sense, as the Jews themselves, or the most cultivated of the Gentiles (iii. 11).

"THE EPISTLE OF PAUL TO PHILEMON"

1. Authorship.—This epistle is thoroughly Pauline; and its contents are of too private and (from a doctrinal and ecclesiastical point of view) too insignificant a nature to have ever been admitted into the Canon if it had not been a genuine writing of Paul's.[1]

---

[1] "It was preserved in the family to which it was addressed, and read first, no doubt, as a precious apostolic message of love and blessing, in the Church which assembled in Philemon's house. Then copies of it became multiplied, and from Colossæ it spread through the Church universal. It is quoted as early as the second century, and has ever, except with some few who question everything, remained an undoubted portion of the writings of St. Paul" (Alford, *How to Study the New Testament*). It was first called in question in the fourth century, on the ground that its matter and contents were beneath the dignity of apostolic authorship!

Its close connection with Colossians has already been referred to. The circumstances under which it reached Philemon, and even the latter's place of residence, would be shrouded in mystery if it were not for Colossians. Yet no hint is given there of the episode in Paul's life which gave rise to this epistle—the only thing relating to it being an allusion to Onesimus as "the faithful and beloved brother who is one of you" (Col. iv. 9). So independent are the two epistles in their contents.

2. The Reader.—"To Philemon our beloved, and fellow-worker."

To ascertain Philemon's residence we have, as already remarked, to consult the Epistle to the Colossians. Philemon himself is not mentioned there; but Archippus whom Paul associates with Philemon and Apphia (probably Philemon's wife) in the opening greeting of this epistle, is mentioned in Colossians in such a way as to imply that he was an office-bearer of the Church either at Colossæ or in the neighbourhood (iv. 17). From the context (iv. 15, 16) it has been suggested that Laodicea, which was about twelve miles from Colossæ, was the scene of Archippus' labours. The association of his name with that of Philemon, in the epistle addressed to the latter, would lead us to suppose that he was either Philemon's son or possibly his minister. The connection of Philemon with Colossæ is further evident from the fact that his slave Onesimus is spoken of in the Epistle to the Colossians as "one of you," and is announced as a visitor to Colossæ (Col. iv. 9) at the same time as he is restored to his master (Philemon 12).

We gather from the epistle that Philemon had been converted to Christianity through the instrumentality of the apostle, and had since then earned a reputation for charity and devotion, his house being one of the meeting-

places of the Church.[1] It was owing to special circumstances, however, that he had the distinction of having
an apostolic letter addressed to him. A slave of his,
Onesimus by name, had absconded (like many another
Phrygian slave) and made his way to Rome, the great
resort of needy adventurers, apparently with the aid of
money stolen from his master. There he was providen-
tially brought under the influence of Paul, and became a
confirmed Christian, endearing himself to the apostle by
his grateful and devoted services in the Gospel. As
Onesimus was Philemon's lawful slave, Paul could not
think of retaining him permanently in his service, so he
took the opportunity afforded by Tychicus' return to
Asia to send him back to his master. In doing so he
gave him this letter to Philemon with the view of
winning for him a merciful reception, and to save him
from the severe and cruel punishment which was permitted by the Roman law—even to the extent of death
—in such cases.[2]

3. **Date and Place of Composition.**—At Rome, 62-63
A.D. (see pp. 108-110).

4. **Character and Contents.**—This is the only letter
of St. Paul addressed to a friend on a matter of private
business that has come down to us, although we cannot
doubt that many others were written by Him which have
not been preserved. On all sides it has received the
warmest praise and admiration—not on account of its
language, which has nothing particular to recommend
it, but for its tact, delicacy, and good feeling. While

---

[1] For similar instances cf. Rom. xvi. 5, 1 Cor. xvi. 19 ; Col. iv. 15.
"There is no clear example of a separate building set apart for
Christian worship within the limits of the Roman empire before the
third century, though apartments in private houses might be specially
devoted to this purpose "(*Lightfoot on Colossians and Philemon*, p. 241).

[2] "The slave was absolutely at his master's disposal ; for the
smallest offence he might be scourged, mutilated, crucified, thrown to
the wild beasts " (*Lightfoot, ibid.* p. 319).

the apostle puts the case very strongly in favour of Onesimus—so strongly that it has been finely said "the word emancipation seems trembling on his lips,"—he refrains from any interference with Philemon's civil rights, seeking only to awaken within him such feelings of humanity and kindness as will be a safeguard against harsh and unbrotherly conduct. In this respect the epistle affords a good illustration of the remedial and reforming influence of the Gospel, which seeks to gain its ends from within and not from without, by persuasion rather than by compulsion.[1]

It has been described as the letter of a Christian gentleman, animated by strong Christian feeling, tempered with discretion, and expressed with dignity and moderation not untouched with humour.[2] The whole tone and structure of the letter was well fitted to bring out the better nature of Philemon ; and it was doubtless to strengthen the appeal—by making Philemon realise that the eyes of his fellow-Christians were upon him— that Paul associates Timothy with himself in his opening greeting, which is addressed not to Philemon alone, but also to other Christian members of his household, and to

---

[1] By teaching the universal brotherhood of men in Jesus Christ, and admitting all alike to full communion in the Church, the apostles brought an influence to bear upon society which could not fail in course of time to lead to the abolition of slavery, and which very soon led to voluntary efforts on the part of congregations to purchase the freedom of their slave-members, as well as to a change of social sentiment with regard to those who remained in slavery. In the measures passed by Constantine, the first Christian Emperor, for ameliorating the condition of slaves, we have the initiation of a movement which was to culminate in the nineteenth century, in the abolition of slavery throughout the British Empire, the liberation of twenty millions of serfs by the Emperor of Russia, the emancipation of the negro in the United States of America, and the final effort to heal "the open sore of the world" in the dark continent of Africa.

[2] In verse 11 there is a play on the name "Onesimus," which in the original means "profitable."

the congregation meeting for worship in his house.   He
also sends salutations from several others whose names
are given at the close, and even throws out a hint that
it may not be long before he visits Philemon in person
(verse 22).   .

CHAPTER XVI

1. Authorship.—As regards external evidence, this is one of the best-attested of Paul's epistles; and until recently its genuineness was never doubted.

Internally it bears a strong resemblance to Colossians, 78 of its 155 verses containing expressions that are also found in that epistle. No doubt the resemblance is due to the fact that the two epistles were written at the same time on kindred subjects to kindred Churches. In both epistles Tychicus is referred to in similar terms as the apostle's messenger; and they both bear to have been written by the apostle while he was a prisoner (vi. 21, 22; Col. iv. 7-9). From the occurrence of the significant word "also" in the parallel passage of this epistle, we may infer that it was written later than the other, although but a few days may have intervened—the closing verses of Colossians (iv. 15-18) having been subsequently added. As might have been expected under the circumstances, the similarity between the two epistles does not extend to continuous passages, but is confined to single verses and occasional expressions such as would be likely to remain in the writer's memory and reappear in his language if he were writing a second time within a very short interval.

We have a remarkable token of the genuineness of this epistle, as of several others attributed to Paul, in the fact that while the writer dwells with great satisfaction on the admission of the Gentiles to the blessings of the Gospel, he expresses himself with regard to it in the language of a patriotic Jew, to whom this expansion of the Messiah's kingdom is a new and marvellous dispensation of divine providence. He speaks with the greatest reverence of the position and privileges of God's ancient people, showing that in a spiritual sense the Gentiles are now raised to an equality with them, and that, in this sense, the rite of circumcision, in particular, is realised in the hearts of all true Christians (ii. 11-20 ; iii. 1-9 ; cf. Col. ii. 11 ; Phil. iii. 2, 3 ; Gal. vi. 16 ; Rom. ii. 28, 29). This is a state of feeling which was most natural in a Jewish-born Christian like Paul, after the struggle against the bondage of the Law, in which he had himself taken a leading part, was practically over.

2. The Readers.—It is now generally agreed that this epistle was not addressed to the Church at Ephesus exclusively, but was of the nature of a circular-letter for the general use of the Churches of Proconsular Asia.[1]

[1] In favour of this supposition are the facts (1) that the words "in Ephesus" (i. 1) were absent from many of the ancient MSS. known to Basil (360 A.D.), and are wanting in the two oldest MSS. that have come down to us (‫א‬ and B) ; (2) that no personal salutations are found in the epistle although Paul had laboured successfully for several years at Ephesus, forming many intimate friendships (Acts xx. 17-38), nor any reference whatever to his experiences during that time ; (3) that he writes as if the Christian graces of his readers were only known to him by report, and as if his apostleship to the Gentiles were only known to them by hearsay (i. 15-19 ; iii. 1-4 ; iv. 17-22 ; cf. Col. i. 3-9) ; (4) that the usual apostolic autograph is absent, owing, we may suppose, to copies of the epistle for the several Churches having to be made out in the course of the messenger's journeys or at the different places at which they had to be delivered. The indirect form of the Benediction at the close of the epistle (vi. 23) : "Peace be to the brethren, and love with faith," is also a corroborative circumstance, being found nowhere else in Paul's epistles ; cf. Col. iv. 18 : "Grace be with you." The great thought of the epistle, too, viz.

There can be little doubt, indeed, that we have here
the epistle referred to in Col. iv. 16, where the apostle
directs the Colossians to read also "the epistle from
Laodicea," and to send their own letter in exchange, for
the benefit of the Christians there.   Even before the
middle of the second century we find a heretical writer
(Marcion) giving this epistle the title "To the Laodiceans."
Yet it is evident that it could not have been specially
addressed to Laodicea, as the apostle sends his salutations
to "the brethren that are in Laodicea" through another
channel (Col. iv. 15).   The difficulty is met by supposing
that we have here a circular-letter of which Laodicea
received a copy in common with other Churches of the
province, — to be communicated to the neighbouring
church at Colossæ.   The name of the Ephesian Church
would naturally become associated with the epistle owing
to its being the leading Church of the district, probably
receiving the first copy from Tychicus when he landed
at its port on his way to Colossæ, and becoming the
source of many later copies to Churches in other parts of
the world.

3. **Date and Place of Composition.**—At Rome, 62-63
A.D. (see pp. 108-110).

4. **Character and Contents.** — It has been said by
Coleridge that this is "one of the divinest compositions
of man.   It embraces every doctrine of Christianity ;
first, those doctrines peculiar to Christianity ; secondly,
those precepts common to it with natural religion."   In
its doctrinal part (i.-iii.) the epistle is distinguished by a
tone of exultation which will not stoop to controversy,
expressing itself in the flow of a sublime eloquence rather
than in the form of a logical argument.   Instead of

the unity of the holy catholic Church, is eminently suitable for such a
letter ; and Asia Minor was rapidly becoming the leading province of
Christendom ; cf. Rev. i. 4 : "John to the seven Churches which are
in Asia."

labouring to demonstrate those truths, regarding the
standing of the Gentiles and his own position as the
apostle of the Gentiles, for which he had contended in
his earlier epistles, the writer takes these things for
granted, and soars into far loftier regions—viewing the
Gospel and the Church in relation not to time, but to
eternity, not to the nations of the world, but to the
universe at large.   Here, as in Colossians, Paul recognises
Christ as the appointed Head of the universe—material
as well as spiritual—and sees in His atoning death the
universal centre of divine providence.   Here, as there,
he is thrilled with a sense of joy not untouched with awe
when he contemplates the great mystery of the divine
will—the eternal purpose of God so long concealed, but
now at length revealed and so far realised through his
instrumentality, to wit, the destined union of Jew and
Gentile in the mystical body of the risen and exalted
Christ.   In this union he sees the pledge and token of
that universal gathering together in one of "all things in
Christ, the things in the heavens, and the things upon the
earth," which is to be the consummation of God's purposes
in Christ (i. 10).   But, whereas in Colossians he dwells
mainly on the person of Christ as the "fulness of the
Godhead bodily," here he is impelled rather to the con-
templation of the *Church* as "the body of Christ, the
fulness of him that filleth all in all," and expatiates
upon the ideal glory and riches of the spiritual blessing
with which its members are blessed in heavenly places
in Christ.[1]

---

[1] The word "spirit" or "spiritual" occurs thirteen times in this
epistle, "the heavenlies" five times, "the grace of God" thirteen
times.   Prof. Findlay (*The Epistles of Paul*, p. 180) suggests that the
"amplitude of style which is a new feature in the apostle's manner as
a writer" was "due perhaps to the leisure of prison and the habit of
meditation which it fostered"; and he points out that it is not
altogether absent from Colossians (i. 9-11, 16-20, 27-29).

The first half of the epistle is thus for the most part a hymn of praise for the grace of God manifested according to His good pleasure which He had purposed in himself, accompanied with the apostle's prayer for his readers that they may realise the glory of their calling. Hence it was Calvin's favourite epistle, as Galatians was of Luther.

In the second part the apostle descends by a swift and beautiful transition to the duties of common life, "I therefore, the prisoner in the Lord, beseech you to walk worthily of the calling wherewith ye were called" (iv. 1). He thus introduces a series of practical exhortations based on the ideal unity of the Church as the harmonious body of Christ, and embracing the various forms of social and domestic duty to which "the new man" is called in the ordinary relations of life. Finally there is a stirring call to put on the whole armour of God for the conflict with the powers of evil, expressed in the language of a metaphor which may have been suggested to Paul by his military surroundings at Rome, and forming a passage of great force and beauty, which of itself would make this epistle a precious heritage of the Church.

The catholic nature of this epistle shows that the apostle's education was well-nigh complete. The Saviour, whom he only knew at his conversion as the Risen One dwelling in another world, has become to him as an all-pervading Presence which may be realised even now in the sphere of common life, as the type of all affection and the centre of all authority, in the State and in the family as well as in the Church.[1] During his residence at Rome, the seat of empire and the centre of the world's secular life, Paul learned, as he had never yet done, the

---

[1] Compare, for example, his view of marriage, the original and central relationship of human life, in this epistle (v. 22-33), and in 1 Cor. (xi.), written about five years before.

meaning of the Saviour's prayer, "Thy kingdom come, Thy will be done on earth as it is in heaven."[1]

[1] "When Paul reached Rome, he began to see after the manner of Rome. The kingdom of God to him took that form which the kingdom of Cæsar assumed to the Latin race—the form of a membership which was connected with all other memberships. . . . What the citizens of the empire beheld merely as a coin bearing the superscription of Cæsar was reflected to his gaze with the stamp and impress of the Son of man. Instead of contemplating, as in days of yore, the dissolution of its life, he began to contemplate the Christianising of its life" (Matheson, *Spiritual Development of St. Paul*).

CHAPTER XVII

1 and 2 Timothy and Titus are known as the Pastoral Epistles, because they relate chiefly to the qualifications and duties of office-bearers entrusted with the pastoral care of the Church.

They are distinguished from all the other epistles of Paul by their want of historical agreement with any period in the life of the apostle as recorded in the Book of Acts, and also by their strongly-marked individuality alike in style and substance. Hence their genuineness has been more called in question than any of the other epistles of Paul—notwithstanding a large amount of external testimony in their favour.

The objections taken to them, however, on those grounds are almost entirely obviated if we suppose them to have been written subsequently to the events narrated in the Book of Acts. This is a supposition that in itself involves no improbability. It was Paul's own expectation (Phil. ii. 24 ; Philemon, ver. 22) that he would be released from the imprisonment in which the Book of Acts leaves him ; and for this expectation he seems to have had sufficient grounds in the inadequacy of the evidence brought against him, as well as in the tolerant attitude of the Roman Government previous to the great

fire in Rome (64 A.D.), which was falsely attributed to
the Christians and brought terrible persecutions in its
train.[1] Moreover, there is an early and general tradition
to the effect that he was released. Assuming that his
liberation did take place, the difficulty of harmonising
the epistles with his life disappears; while the late date
of their composition — possibly some years after his
release — would go far to account for the peculiarity
of their contents. It is no wonder that questions of
discipline and government as well as of orthodoxy
should now receive from the apostle a larger measure of
attention than they had done hitherto, considering the
growing needs of the Church, arising from the gradual
expansion of its organisations as a corporate body held
together by a common creed. The Church had now
been for many years a visible institution with office-
bearers of its own; and important doctrines had been
vindicated and established. To conserve these doctrines
and to provide for the regular superintendence of the
Church after he and the other apostles had passed away,
was Paul's great object in writing these epistles.[2]

The idea that the epistles may have been the products
of a later age is in many respects untenable. Both as
regards the office-bearers mentioned, namely, bishops
and deacons, and the doctrinal needs and dangers of the

[1] "If Paul's trial had resulted in conviction and punishment, it
would have formed a precedent which must have been followed in
other cases for a considerable time previous to 64 A.D.—all the more
so because he was a Roman citizen. But this is inconsistent with the
statements of Tacitus" (Prof. Ramsay, *Expositor*, July 1893).

[2] The large infusion of new words (*i.e.* words not elsewhere used
by the apostle) is in accordance with the gradual expansion of his
vocabulary, which is evident on a comparison of Paul's successive
writings; and, in particular, many of these words are new simply
because the things they signify had not previously come within the
scope of the apostle's teaching. For it must be remembered that the
Pastoral Epistles differ widely from the other writings of St. Paul
alike as regards their recipients—friends and colleagues, not congregations—and the ecclesiastical questions with which they deal.

Church, they remind us far more of the state of things existing during Paul's first imprisonment at Rome, when he wrote Philippians and Colossians, than of anything in the second century. By the latter time the name of "bishop" had been appropriated to a chief dignitary ruling over the "presbyters" or elders, instead of being applied as here to the presbyters themselves as the overseers of the congregation (Titus i. 5, 7, cf. Acts xx. 17-28).

Moreover, the "knowledge falsely so called" which is denounced in these epistles comes far short of the elaborate Gnosticism of the second century, which set itself in direct opposition to the orthodox faith, and repudiated all affinity with the Jewish law.[1]

"THE FIRST EPISTLE OF PAUL THE APOSTLE
TO TIMOTHY"

1. Authorship. — The strong external evidence in favour of the genuineness of this epistle has been already mentioned. We can hear echoes of its language as far back as the close of the first century. A hundred years later we find it universally accepted as Paul's, although it had been rejected in the course of the second century by one or two heretical writers,[2] owing to the difficulty of reconciling its teaching with their favourite tenets.

In a general sense its peculiarities in language and

---

[1] The errors which the apostle here combats are evidently of a vague and unformed character, awaiting further development, as he indicates by his references to the future ; and in particular they bear traces of that semi-Jewish character which we know to have belonged to Christian Gnosticism in its earlier stages. In this respect, as well as in the morbid asceticism professed by the false teachers, the corrupt form of Christianity that meets us here is very similar to that which is dealt with in the Epistle to the Colossians,—but exhibited in a somewhat ranker growth.

[2] Marcion and Basilides.

contents have also been accounted for. In some respects,
however, these peculiarities are positively in favour of
the Pauline authorship. How unlikely that a forger
should have inserted the word "mercy"[1] (i. 2) in the
usual Pauline greeting "grace and peace," or have omitted
to make frequent use of the connecting particles "therefore," "wherefore," "then," "as," etc., which are so
common in Paul's writings.

Objection has been taken to the expression "let no
man despise thy youth" (iv. 12), as if the apostle could
not have applied that language to Timothy when he
may have been a man of thirty-five years of age. But
we have here rather a token of genuineness. For youth
is relative; and in Paul's eyes Timothy, being so much
his junior, and having been known to him as a lad,
would naturally seem young,—especially in view of his
great responsibilities in being set over so many elders.[2]

[1] This remark applies also to 2 Tim. (i. 2) and Titus (i. 4).

[2] Equally groundless is the objection that Paul had predicted to
the Ephesian elders that "he should see their face no more" (Acts
xx. 25), whereas this epistle implies that he had recently paid them
another visit. For the words quoted contain the expression of a presentiment or at most of a conviction, not of an inspired prophecy, on
the part of the apostle; and, besides, the language of the epistle, "as
I exhorted thee to tarry at Ephesus when I was going into Macedonia,"
does not necessarily imply that the writer himself had been at Ephesus.
It is quite possible he may have exhorted Timothy by a message from
a distance, or have met him at Miletus as he had met the Ephesian
elders several years before.

Again it has been argued that the instructions contained in this
epistle might have been more easily given by the apostle in person
during his recent visit to Ephesus, or on the subsequent visit to which
he was still looking forward (iii. 14). But this latter visit was regarded by the apostle as very uncertain (iii. 15); while the former
one, as we have seen, is a very doubtful inference from i. 3. Even
if it be true, however, that the apostle had recently been at Ephesus,
there is nothing improbable in the supposition that it was in consequence of what he then learned of the condition of the Church, and
as the result of subsequent reflection, that he was led to furnish
Timothy with these rules and directions in a written form, which
could be of permanent service, and if necessary might be referred to
in the hearing of the congregation.

2. The Reader.—"Unto Timothy, my true child in faith." The disciple thus addressed was one of the apostle's converts, and became his dearest friend and coadjutor in the closing years of his life. Of a pious Jewish family by the mother's side—his father was a Greek—he received a strict religious training in the scriptures of the Old Testament (Acts xvi. 1 ; 2 Tim. i. 1-5 ; iii. 14, 15). He seems to have been converted to Christianity during Paul's first visit to Lystra and Derbe; for, on the apostle's second visit to that quarter about three years afterwards, Timothy was a disciple so well reported of by the brethren at Lystra and Iconium as to be deemed worthy of being associated with Paul as a labourer in the Gospel (Acts xvi. 1, 2 ; 1 Tim. i. 2 ; 2 Tim. iii. 10, 11, cf. Acts xiv. 9-21). To this position he was duly ordained by the laying on of hands, after being circumcised to render him more acceptable to the Jews (Acts xvi. 3 ; 1 Tim. vi. 12 ; iv. 14 ; 2 Tim. i. 6). Thereafter we find him constantly associated with the apostle either as his companion or as his delegate to Churches at a distance —although his influence seems to have been somewhat weakened by a certain timidity and softness of disposition. He was with the apostle during his first imprisonment at Rome, being associated with him in three of the four epistles which Paul then wrote (Phil., Col., and Philemon). From this epistle we gather that after the apostle's release Timothy was left for a time in charge of the Church at Ephesus; and it was while in this trying and responsible position that he received the two epistles that bear his name.

3. Date and Place of Composition.—The first epistle seems to have been sent to Timothy from Macedonia under the circumstances referred to in i. 3 ; but whether before or after Paul's intended visits to Philippi (Phil. ii. 24), Colossæ (Philemon, ver. 22), and Spain—which,

according to an ancient tradition originating in the first
century, he did visit (Rom. xv. 24)—it is quite impossible to say.   Various routes have been sketched by
which Paul may have travelled after his release from
Rome, comprising visits to .the places just mentioned
and also to Ephesus, Crete (Tit. i. 5), Nicopolis (Tit. iii.
12), and Troas (2 Tim. iv. 13); but they are all more or
less conjectural.   While it is impossible to ascertain the
precise movements of the apostle after his release, or the
exact year in which this epistle was written, we may
safely place its composition between 64 A.D., the year
after Paul's release, and 67 A.D., shortly before his death,
—the date usually assigned to the latter being 68 A.D.,
the last year of Nero, under whom, according to the
general tradition, Paul suffered martyrdom.   The most
probable date is 67 A.D., which gives an interval of
several years to account for the change in the apostle's
style and in the condition of the Church, and makes the
three pastoral epistles very nearly contemporaneous.

4. Character and Contents.—These have been already
indicated in the general remarks at pp. 132, 133.   The
epistle is partly official, partly personal.   While addressed
to Timothy individually, it contains Paul's apostolic instructions to guide him in the work of supervision
assigned to him at Ephesus (i. 1-4).   The anticipations
of evil which Paul had expressed to the Ephesian elders
at Miletus (Acts. xx. 29, 30) had already in some measure
been realised, and there was great need for wisdom in
the rulers of the Church.   It is not easy to trace any
regular sequence in the topics discussed; but the contents of the epistle may be summarised as follows :—

The folly and danger of the Judaic fancies with which
false teachers were overlaying the Gospel (i.); exhortations to catholicity of spirit as well as to reverence and
decorum in acts of worship (ii.); the qualifications re-

quisite in the office-bearers of the Church (bishops and deacons), and the need for fidelity and care on their part in view of the increasing corruption (iii.) ; counsels regarding Timothy's treatment of the elders and other classes in the congregation (iv.-v.) ; cautions against covetousness, and exhortations to the rich to make a good use of their means,—concluding with an appeal to Timothy to guard that which was committed to his trust, and to avoid "profane babblings, and oppositions of the knowledge which is falsely so called " (vi.).

Although in some respects on a humbler level intellectually than most of Paul's writings, and bearing traces of the writer's advancing years, this epistle contains not a few golden texts to be held in everlasting remembrance.[1]

---

[1] i. 5, 15 ; ii. 3-6 ; iii. 16 ; vi. 6, 10, 12.

CHAPTER XVIII

"THE EPISTLE OF PAUL TO TITUS"

1. Authorship.—To the general remarks at pp. 132, 133 we may add the following notes of genuineness :—

(1) The quotation made from Epimenides in i. 12 is in accordance with the manner of St. Paul, who is the only New Testament writer that quotes heathen authors (Acts xvii. 28 ; 1 Cor. xv. 33). At the same time the use of the word "prophet" in this passage, as compared with "poet" in the quotation reported in Acts xvii. 28, is against the supposition of imitation.

(2) The introduction of such unknown names as Artemas and Zenas, as well as of Nicopolis (iii. 12, 13), which are mentioned nowhere else in the New Testament, and the unique designation of the apostle himself (i. 1), are at variance with the idea of forgery.

2. The Reader.—"To Titus, my true child after a common faith" (i. 4). Judging from the allusions to Titus in Paul's epistles [1] he seems to have been the ablest and most reliable of all the friends and coadjutors whom the apostle had about him in his later years. As an uncircumcised Gentile who had been converted by Paul, he

---

[1] In the Book of Acts Titus is never mentioned.

represented in his own person the breadth and freedom of the Gospel, for which the apostle had so zealously and successfully contended.

The conversion of Titus had taken place at a comparatively early period in the apostle's ministry, for he accompanied Paul and Barnabas on their visit from Antioch to Jerusalem to vindicate the freedom of the Gentiles from the ceremonial law of the Jews (Gal. ii. 1-4). We find him figuring prominently at another crisis in the apostle's ministry, when the strife and confusion in the Corinthian Church threatened to destroy St. Paul's influence. His remarkable success in the difficult mission then assigned to him (p. 82), which called for the exercise of combined firmness and tact, and from which Apollos appears to have shrunk (1 Cor. xvi. 12), marked him out as an able and trustworthy delegate, and explains his selection ten years later for the important and difficult position which he temporarily held in Crete when this letter was addressed to him.

Of the state of the Church in Crete we know very little except what may be gathered from this epistle. In all probability the Gospel had been first brought to the island by those of its inhabitants who witnessed the outpouring of the spirit on the day of Pentecost ("Cretans," Acts ii. 11). More than thirty years had passed since then, and there were now, probably, quite a number of congregations in the island, which was a hundred and forty miles long and was famous for its hundred cities.

Paul had been there once before, on his way from Cæsarea to Rome; but being a prisoner at the time he could have had little or no opportunity of preaching. It may have been on that occasion, however, that he. saw the necessity for organising the various congregations, as he was now seeking to do through the instrumentality of

Titus. It was a difficult task, for the Cretans bore a
bad character. "Liars, evil beasts, idle gluttons," was
the description which had been given of them long
before by "one of themselves" (Epimenides, 600 B.C.)—
a testimony confirmed by several other ancient writers.
They were a mixed population of Greeks and Asiatics,
with a considerable infusion of Jews. To the influence
of these latter, acting on native superstition, the corruption of Christian doctrine, of which we hear in the epistle,
appears to have been largely due (i. 10, 14 ; iii. 9).[1]

3. **Date and Place of Composition.** — The striking
resemblance of this epistle to 1 Timothy justifies us in
assigning it to the same year (say 67 A.D.). It may have
been written in Asia Minor when the apostle was on his
way to Nicopolis.

4. **Character and Contents.**—Although addressed to
a friend, this letter, like 1 Timothy, has to a certain
extent an official character. This is evident from the
greeting : "Paul, a servant of God, and an apostle of
Jesus Christ . . . " (i. 1-4). It was intended to furnish
Titus, as the apostle's representative in Crete, with the
same assistance in his work as had already been rendered
to Timothy. From i. 5 it would appear that the apostle
had heard of opposition being offered to Titus, and
desired to strengthen his hands for his arduous under-
taking. With this view he gives him directions for the
appointment of properly-qualified presbyters [2] in every
city, who should be able and willing to teach "the
sound doctrine," and to counteract the useless and un-

---

[1] In the subsequent history of the island, Titus has figured prominently as the patron-saint of the community.

[2] It is remarkable that in this epistle there is no mention of the
other class of office-bearers, the deacons, who figure so largely in
1 Timothy. This would be unaccountable if the two epistles were
cunningly devised forgeries proceeding from the same hand in the
interests of ecclesiastical order.

warrantable speculations of a semi-Jewish character, involving endless controversy, which were propagated by dishonest self-seeking teachers. He also reminds Titus of suitable exhortations to be addressed to the various classes in the Church, for the promotion of that practical godliness which ought to accompany sound doctrine. Titus himself is admonished to show himself in all things " an ensample of good works."

The epistle contains a number of memorable sayings, including some of the most comprehensive statements of Christian truth to be found in the New Testament (ii. 11-14 ; iii. 4-7). In ii. 11-14 we have an excellent illustration of the "doctrine which is according to godliness," that sober-minded union of faith and practice, which is the ripest fruit of Christianity, and which forms the chief burden of this most salutary letter.

The epistle concludes with some allusions to personal matters (iii. 12-15), in the course of which Paul bids Titus come to him at Nicopolis as soon as Artemas or Tychicus has arrived to relieve him. This is scarcely consistent with the view of some Episcopalian writers that Titus held a permanent official position in the island.

" THE SECOND EPISTLE OF PAUL THE APOSTLE TO TIMOTHY "

1. Authorship.—In several passages this epistle bears the stamp of genuineness as a writing of St. Paul's, notably at i. 5-18 and iv. 9-22. In particular the opening thanksgiving (i. 3) is characteristic of Paul, eight of his other letters having a similar commencement, which is not to be found in any of the other epistles of the New Testament. At the same time this is not such a prominent feature as to lead to imitation ; and, as a matter of fact, it is not found in the two other Pastoral Epistles.

A strong proof of genuineness is afforded by the proper names (of Church members) in the epistle. They are twenty-three in number, including ten mentioned elsewhere, exclusive of Paul and Timothy. In connection with several of these ten, remarks are made which a forger would have been very unlikely to invent. *E.g.* " Demas forsook me, having loved this present world " (iv. 10, cf. Col. iv. 14), is more like what we should have expected to find concerning Mark, in view of his former desertion of Paul (Acts xiii. 13) ; whereas we find favourable mention of him in this epistle (iv. 11). Dalmatia is also a strange place to have invented as a destination for Titus (iv. 10), considering that he had been written to so recently at Crete—although it fits in with the summons to Nicopolis which had been previously addressed to him. A striking argument has been derived from the occurrence of the name *Linus* in the closing salutations. The argument is based on the fact that Linus, Cletus, and Clement are the names of the first three "bishops" of the Church of Rome, preserved in her Eucharistic Service, dating from the second century. If the epistle had been written in the post-apostolic age, Linus, it is held, would have been sure to receive a more prominent place in the list of salutations, and his name would have been accompanied with that of Cletus, or at all events with that of Clement, as the latter was believed to have been an immediate disciple of Paul.

Altogether, the personal details contained in this epistle, especially in its closing chapter, are so unusually abundant, that it would have been comparatively easy of detection if it had been a forgery. As it is, the marks of genuineness are so numerous and striking, and there is such a tone of sincerity and earnestness running through the whole epistle, that it is accepted by many critics who reject its two companions. But, as the main

objections to the latter, on the score of their novel language
and teaching, and their want of correspondence with the
Book of Acts, apply equally to 2 Timothy, it is generally
admitted that the three epistles must stand or fall together.
Hence any argument for the Pauline authorship of this
epistle has a reflex influence on that of the two others.

2. The Reader.—"To Timothy, my beloved child"
(i. 2), see p. 136.

3. Date and Place of Composition.—From i. 8, 16-18,
it is evident that this epistle was written by Paul while
a prisoner at Rome.   That it was a different imprisonment from that mentioned in Acts xxviii. may be inferred
not only from the general considerations adduced on
pp. 132, 133, but more particularly from the apostle's
anticipation of a fatal result (iv. 6-8) as compared with his
expectation of release in Phil. ii. 24 and Philemon, ver. 22.[1]

---

[1] There are several other circumstances, however, which lead us to
the same conclusion. (1) The difference between Paul's position
during his first imprisonment (Acts xxviii. 30, 31 ; Phil. i. 12-14),
and at the time he wrote this epistle (ii. 9 ; i. 15-17 ; iv. 16). (2)
The absence of Timothy, Demas, and Mark (iv. 10, 11), of whom the
first-named is associated with the apostle in the epistles to Philippians,
Colossians, and Philemon, and the two latter are mentioned in Colossians as sending salutations (Col. iv. 10, 14). (3) The statement in
this epistle, "Erastus abode at Corinth ; but Trophimus I left at
Miletus sick " (iv. 20).   For in the apostle's last recorded journey to
Jerusalem Trophimus was not left at Miletus, but went with the
apostle all the way to Jerusalem (Acts xx. 1-4, 15 ; xxi. 29); and
as for Erastus' stay in Corinth, we know that Timothy was one of
Paul's companions (Acts xx. 1-4) during the same journey, after the
apostle's last recorded visit to Greece, and could not have required
to be informed that "Erastus abode in Corinth," if that had been the
occasion referred to.   In his subsequent voyage from Cæsarea to Rome,
as recorded in the closing chapters of Acts, it is certain that the
apostle visited neither Miletus nor Corinth.   (4) The request here
made to Timothy : "The cloke that I left at Troas with Carpus,
bring when thou comest, and the books, especially the parchments"
(iv. 13).   For there was an interval of several years between Paul's
last recorded visit to Troas and his first imprisonment at Rome.   A
subsequent visit, however, after his release, would fit in with the fresh
journey from Miletus to Corinth, which seems to be implied in the
remark above made (3).

Such a second imprisonment was in itself not at all unlikely after the great fire in 64 A.D., when the Christian religion was put under the ban ; and we know the apostle had no lack of enemies to give information against him. If we are right in dating the first epistle 67 A.D., we may assign this one to 67-68 A.D.

4. Character and Contents. — We have here the apostle's last will and testament in favour of the Church, in the form of a farewell charge to his beloved child Timothy. He still hoped to see him once again, and repeatedly urges him to do his best to come to him shortly—"before winter," while navigation is still practicable (iv. 9, 21). His yearning for Timothy's society in his lonely prison reminds us of our Lord's desire for the sympathy and prayers of His disciples on the eve of His Passion ; and in this epistle, as in our Lord's teaching during the week preceding His death, there is blended with a sublime confidence in the speaker's own future, dark foreboding of approaching trial and temptation for the Church. He warns Timothy of the "grievous times" to come (iii. 1), and exhorts him to adhere steadfastly to the teaching he had received from the apostle on the foundation of the Scripture "inspired of God," and to take security for such teaching being continued by "faithful men who shall be able to teach others also" —bidding Timothy emulate his own example in the endurance of hardship and in the practice of self-denial for the sake of the Gospel.

A peculiarity of this as of the other pastoral epistles is the introduction of short and weighty statements with the words, "Faithful is the saying." In ii. 11-13 we have what is probably part of a Christian hymn, expressing the faith in which the apostle would have Timothy to meet his trials.

CHAPTER XIX

1. Authorship.—This is a question which cannot be answered with any degree of certainty. The earliest witness on the subject is Pantænus of Alexandria, in the latter half of the second century, who assigned the epistle, as Eusebius tells us, to the Apostle Paul. In keeping with this opinion we find that the Eastern Church generally regarded it as the work of Paul; but some of the most learned of its bishops and teachers were constrained by internal evidence to depart somewhat from the traditional view. Their idea was that Paul might have written the original, and one of his disciples have translated it into Greek; or that the apostle might have supplied the thoughts, and some disciple have put them into words. In this sense Origen maintains that the thoughts were worthy of the apostle, but "who it was that wrote the epistle, God only knows certainly."

The opinion of the Western Church was for a long time adverse to the Pauline authorship. Clement of Rome, who wrote before the close of the first century, frequently quotes the epistle, but never claims for it the authority of Paul. If he believed that the epistle was written by Paul, it is difficult to account for the ignorance of the Roman Church on the subject in succeeding generations—all the more so because of the connection of the epistle with Italy (xiii. 24). It was not till the close of the fourth century, and in spite of its traditions to the contrary, that the Western Church accepted the epistle as a writing of Paul's.[1]

Even if the external testimony in favour of the Pauline authorship were much stronger than it is, a study of the style and structure of the book would compel us to adopt a different view. Instead of the rugged, impetuous, and occasionally disjointed style of the apostle, we have here polished diction and carefully-constructed sentences. "The movement of this writer resembles that of an oriental sheikh with his robes of honour wrapped around him; the movement of St. Paul is that of an athlete girded for the race. The eloquence of this writer, even when it is at its most majestic volume, resembles the flow of a river; the rhetoric of St. Paul is like the rush of a mountain torrent amid opposing rocks." In addition to this general dissimilarity of style there are so many well-marked differences in detail,[2] that the idea that Paul wrote this epistle has now been generally aban-

[1] But it is interesting to observe that the Westminster Confession does not include it among St. Paul's epistles.

[2] (1) There is in this epistle a marked absence of the opening salutation and thanksgiving usual with St. Paul.

(2) There is an acknowledgment on the part of the writer that he and his readers were indebted in some measure for their knowledge of the Gospel to "them that heard" the Lord (ii. 3), whereas Paul repudiated for himself any such dependence on the testimony of others (Gal. i. 11-17).

(3) In quoting from the Old Testament the writer of this epistle makes use of such phrases as "God saith," "the Holy Spirit saith," "he testifieth," which are not found in St. Paul's writings.

(4) He invariably quotes from the Septuagint in its Alexandrian MS., without regard to the Hebrew, whereas Paul often corrects the Septuagint by the Hebrew, and when he quotes from the Greek version, follows the text found in the Vatican MS.

(5) He never designates the Saviour as "our Lord Jesus Christ" or "Christ Jesus our Lord" (expressions which occur nearly seventy

doned.   Nor can we even regard it as the translation of
a Hebrew work of the apostle's, which was a conjecture
of Clement of Alexandria.   Not only is it possessed of
such a rhetorical grace and finish as is scarcely attainable
in a translation, but in several other respects it bears
unmistakable tokens of having been originally written in
Greek.[1]   But although we cannot assign the epistle to
St. Paul, this need not impair our sense of its value as
an acknowledged portion of the New Testament.   Its
value is independent of its human authorship.   "If it
should be found that a noble picture which had been
attributed to Raphael was not by that artist, there would
not be one masterpiece the less, but one great master
the more " (*Thiersch*).

While the evidence is conclusive against the epistle
having been written by Paul, there is yet reason to
believe that it was the work of one of Paul's school.
The writer appears to have been acquainted with some
of Paul's epistles,[2] and he uses many words which are
found nowhere in the New Testament except in Paul's
writings, or in his speeches as reported by Luke.   He
also refers to Timothy as a personal friend—although in
different terms from those used by the apostle (xiii. 23).

By which of Paul's friends or associates the letter was
written it is difficult to say.   Neither Clement nor Luke

times in Paul's epistles), but generally speaks of Him as "Jesus," or
"Christ," or "the Lord."

(6) Greek particles of frequent occurrence in Paul's writings are
entirely absent from this epistle ; while some are found here that are
never used by Paul.

[1] It has numerous plays on Greek words, and contains expressions
that have no equivalent in Hebrew ; it makes its Old Testament
quotations direct from the Septuagint, in some cases even building an
argument on forms of expression which do not occur in the Hebrew
text.

[2] Cf. ii. 8 and 1 Cor. xv. 27 ; ii. 10 and Rom. xi. 36 ; ii. 14, 2
Tim. i. 10 and 1 Cor. xv. 26 ; v. 12-14 and 1 Cor. iii. 2 ; vi. 10 and
1 Thess. i. 3 ; x. 30 and Rom. xii. 19 ; xii. 14 and Rom. xii. 18.

(whose names were suggested as early as the third century) can be credited with the work, so greatly do their styles differ from that of the epistle. Luther's conjecture that Apollos may have been the writer is favoured by the description of the latter in Acts xviii. 24-28, viewed in connection with the internal characteristics of the epistle, and it has been widely accepted. But if Apollos was the writer, it is difficult to account for the complete disappearance of his name from the traditions of the Church, more especially in the East.

There is another name, in itself not at all an improbable one, for which we have the authority of Tertullian of Carthage, who wrote in the beginning of the third century. That presbyter refers to Barnabas as the author of the epistle, in terms which would imply that this was no new supposition; and his testimony is all the more important because he had been at one time resident in Rome and knew what was the current belief of the Church there. In many respects the name of Barnabas answers the requirements of the case. As a Jewish Christian who enjoyed the confidence of the apostles and was on intimate terms with the Church at Jerusalem, of which he had been an early benefactor; as a Levite, familiar with the usages and customs of the Jewish sanctuary; as a native, and frequent visitor, of Cyprus, sufficiently acquainted with Hellenistic literature to be able to preach to Hellenists, and at one time (according to an ancient tradition) a teacher, like his nephew Mark, at Alexandria, with which Cyprus was closely connected; as a good man full of the Holy Ghost and of faith, whose surname of Barnabas, "son of exhortation" (conferred on him by the apostles), marked him out as a man of great persuasive influence :—in all these respects this Church-leader was well fitted to be the writer of a "word of exhortation" (xiii. 22)—in the Greek language and after the Alexandrian mode of thought—to the wavering and distracted Hebrews (Acts iv. 36, 37; ix. 26, 27; xi. 19-30; xiii. 1; xv. 39).

2. The Readers.—"To the Hebrews." We have no reason to doubt that this part of the superscription—which probably formed the whole of the original, and is of immemorial antiquity—gives a correct indication of the readers for whom the epistle was intended. The whole tenor of the epistle implies that it was written for Jewish Christians. But various allusions show that it was not intended merely for Hebrew Christians in general, but for some definite community (v. 11, 12; vi. 9, 10; x. 32-34; xiii. 1, 7, 19, 23). Which of the Hebrew communities, in particular, is addressed has been much disputed. Alexandria, Antioch, Ephesus, Rome, have all been suggested. Something may be said for each of them, especially Antioch;[1] but from the way in which the Gentiles are entirely ignored in the epistle—the word "people," which frequently occurs, being always used to designate the Jews—it would seem most probable that the letter was intended for Christians in Jerusalem or in some other part of Palestine. It was only in Palestine that Churches were to be found entirely composed of Jewish Christians; and the troubles that overtook these congregations soon afterwards in connection with the destruction of Jerusalem would go far to account for the ignorance and uncertainty of the early Church as to the authorship and the original destination of this epistle—an oblivion that is otherwise difficult to explain. Moreover, it was in Palestine that the temptations to relapse into Judaism, against which the writer is so anxious to guard his readers, were most formidable. The

---

[1] The language of xii. 4, however, "Ye have not yet resisted unto blood," could hardly have been addressed to Christians at Rome after 64 A.D.

sacerdotal splendour of the ancient sanctuary threw into
the shade the simple forms of Christian worship; and
the flames of patriotic zeal burned more fiercely in the
Holy Land than among the Jews of the Dispersion. The
Hebrew Christians residing there must have felt themselves more and more under the necessity of choosing
between their country and their faith, between a revolt
against the Romans and a patient waiting for the coming
of the Saviour. Exposed to persecution and excom-
munication at the hands of their fanatical and exasperated
countrymen, deeply attached to the religion of their
fathers and with a strong love of outward ceremonial,
disappointed by the delay of the Second Coming and by
the rejection of the Gospel on the part of so many of
their kindred, they stood in urgent need of the consola-
tions and the warnings which are addressed to them in
this epistle.

3. Date and Place of Composition.—The only clue
to guide us as to the place of writing is to be found
in the message at the close of the epistle: "They
of Italy salute you." This may either mean that the
writer was sending greetings from the Church in Italy,
or from Italian Christians resident in some foreign
city from which he wrote. The latter would be quite
natural and intelligible if the epistle was going to some
Church in Italy, whose members were receiving a special
greeting from their countrymen abroad. But, as we
have seen, the epistle had probably a different destination; and we may therefore conclude that it was written
from some place in Italy—the more so as it informs its
readers of Timothy's liberation, which took place presumably at Rome, whither he had been summoned by St. Paul
in his last imprisonment (xiii. 23; 2 Tim. iv. 9, 21).

On this supposition the date of the epistle would be
about 68 A.D., which tallies with other indications of

time in the epistle.   That it was written before the Fall
of Jerusalem is evident not only from the allusions to
the sacrificial system as still going on (x. 2, 3, etc.) and
to the old covenant as "becoming old" and "nigh unto
vanishing away" (viii. 13), but still more perhaps from
the absence of any allusion to the destruction of the
Temple.   That event, if it had already occurred, would
have rendered superfluous any other proof of the transitory and imperfect nature of the Old Testament
dispensation.

4. Character and Contents.—In many respects this
book has more of the character of a treatise than of a
letter.   Its great theme is the superiority of Christianity
to Judaism.   This superiority it proves not so much
by minimising the old covenant—which Paul had been
obliged to do in vindicating the freedom of his Gentile
converts—as by magnifying the new in the sense of its
being a fulfilment of the old.

The epistle may be divided into two parts, the first
mainly of an argumentative or expository character
(i.–x. 18), the second chiefly hortatory and practical
(x. 19–xiii.).

(1) In the former the writer seeks to establish the
supremacy of Christ and of the Christian Dispensation.
After the opening statement (i. 1-3) as to the divine
revelation being completed and concentrated in the
"Son," he proceeds to show His superiority to the
angels, through whom the Law was believed to have
been given (i.-ii), to Moses (iii.), and to Joshua (iv.).
But his main efforts are directed to proving Christ's
superiority and that of His religion to the sacerdotal
system of the Jews.   In v.-vii. he shows that Christ,
while possessing in common with Aaron all the qualifications of a true priest, belongs to a higher order of
priesthood, represented not by Aaron but by Melchizedek.

In the story of the meeting of Melchizedek with Abraham
(Gen. xiv. 18-20) and in the Psalmist's prophetic allusion
to the former (Ps. cx. 4) he finds many reasons of an
allegorical nature to justify this view. He represents
the Head of the Christian Church as the possessor of an
unchangeable priesthood, secured by the divine oath—
not transitory, but permanent—exercised not on earth
but in heaven—constituted "not after the law of a carnal
commandment, but after the power of an endless life."
In viii.–x. 18, a similar superiority is proved to belong to
the Christian Dispensation, with its law written on the
heart, and its sacrifice offered "once for all" in a "tabernacle not made with hands," whereby Christ hath "through
his own blood" "obtained eternal redemption."

(2) In the course of the argument occasional exhortations and warnings are introduced (ii. 1-4 ; iii. 7-13 ; iv.
11-16 ; v. 12–vi. 20). But the practical application is
mainly reserved for the concluding chapters, x. 19–xiii.
After exhorting his readers to avail themselves of the
"new and living way" which has been thus consecrated
for them into "the holy place," and warning them
against the terrible consequences of apostasy, he com-
forts their hearts with the assurance that though they
may be disowned by the sacerdotal leaders at Jerusalem,
they are in the true line of fellowship with the saints
and holy men of old, whose devotion had been shown, not
by the observance of an outward ceremonial, but by faith
in the unseen (xi.). In the next chapter, after exhorting
them to patience under their trials through the sustaining
power of God's fatherly love, he introduces a striking
contrast between the terrors of Sinai and the attractive
glories of Mount Zion. In the last chapter (xiii.) he
gives a number of salutary counsels and admonitions, in
the course of which he calls upon his readers to go forth
unto Jesus "without the camp, bearing his reproach,"

as Jesus Himself "suffered without the gate." He exhorts them to offer the sacrifices of praise and well-doing which are required of the Christian, and bids them render obedience to their ecclesiastical superiors. The epistle concludes with a request for their prayers on behalf of the writer, that he "may be restored to (them) the sooner," followed by a beautiful benediction, and a few last words of personal explanation and greeting.

CHAPTER XX

THERE are seven epistles which from the fourth century have gone under the name of the Catholic (or General) Epistles, viz. James; 1 and 2 Peter; 1, 2, 3 John; and Jude. They were so called in contradistinction to Paul's epistles, which, with the exception of the Pastoral Epistles and Philemon, are addressed to individual Churches, also seven in number. In most of the Greek MSS. the Catholic Epistles stand next to the Book of Acts, although they were much later than the epistles of Paul in obtaining general recognition in the Church.

"THE GENERAL EPISTLE OF JAMES"[1]

1. Authorship.—In common with four other of the Catholic Epistles, viz. 2 Peter, 2 and 3 John, and Jude, this epistle is described by Eusebius (about 325 A.D.) as a disputed book of the New Testament, in the sense of not being universally acknowledged by the Church.

In the fourth century the claims of these and other writings to a place in the New Testament Canon were carefully sifted, the result being to vindicate the character of each of the disputed epistles (as appears from the

---

[1] The Hebrew original of this name is Jacob.

Decrees of the Council of Laodicea, 364 A.D., and of
Carthage, 397 A.D.), while a number of other books
which, although not in the New Testament, had been
read in church along with them were finally disallowed.

With regard to the Epistle of James in particular the
rarity of allusions to it in the early Christian writers[1]
may be accounted for by its circulation being confined to
Jewish Christians, as well as by the narrow sphere of
labour in which the writer himself moved, his life
apparently having been entirely spent in Jerusalem.

The internal evidence of the book is strongly in its
favour, and it is now generally admitted to be a genuine
work of "James, the Lord's brother" (Gal. i. 19), who
presided for many years over the Church at Jerusalem.
(1) The writer's modest designation of himself—"James,
a servant of God and of the Lord Jesus Christ," is against
the idea of forgery.   (2) The epistle was evidently
written for Jewish Christians by one of themselves.[2]   It
speaks of Abraham as "our father" (ii. 21); it calls the
readers' place of worship "your synagogue" (ii. 2, R.V.),
it calls God "the Lord of Sabaoth" (v. 4); it takes for
granted an acquaintance with Old Testament characters
(ii. 25; v. 10, 17); it alludes to Jewish forms of oath
(v. 12); it refers to "the law" as still binding (ii. 8-11;
iv. 11); and it contains no allusions to those sins of the
flesh which figure so prominently in epistles designed for
Gentile readers.   (3) It bears traces of having been

---

[1] The earliest express quotation from this epistle is found in the
writings of Origen ; but the language of Clement of Rome, and still
more clearly of Hermas, would lead us to believe that it was known to
these writers. Still more significant is the fact that it has a place in
the ancient Syriac Version (the Peschito).

[2] Although written in comparatively pure Greek (owing, it may be,
to our epistle being the translation of an Aramaic original by a com-
petent Greek scholar acting under the direction of James), its literary
character as a whole is essentially Hebrew, reminding us of the Book
of Proverbs and other Jewish writings.

written by a native of Palestine—in its allusions to "the
scorching wind" (i. 11), the sea (i. 6; iii. 4), "sweet
water and bitter" (the latter referring to the brackish
springs of the country, iii. 11, 12); the vine, olive, and
fig (iii. 12); "the early and latter rain" (v. 7). (4)
It shows a familiar acquaintance with Christ's teaching,
although its language is not such as to betray an imitation of our Gospels.[1] (5) It reflects a state of Jewish
society—the rich oppressing the poor—which is described
by Josephus and other Jewish writers as prevailing in
the period succeeding the death of our Lord, but which
in a great manner ceased to exist after the rebellion that
terminated in the destruction of Jerusalem.

With regard to the author's personal history the
following points may be noted. He and his brothers
Joses, Simon, and Jude (Matt. xiii. 55; Mark vi. 3) were
either the children of Joseph and Mary, and younger
brothers of our Lord, or else they were the children of
Joseph by a former marriage. The latter supposition
seems the more probable, both because it is in harmony
with the earliest traditions of antiquity, and because it
helps to explain the attitude of James and his brothers
towards Jesus during His lifetime (Matt. xii. 46 and John
vii. 3-5), and the committal of Mary to the keeping, not
of her stepsons, but of the Apostle John (John xix. 26).
We find that at an advanced period in our Lord's ministry
His brethren did not believe in Him (John vii. 5); but
immediately after the Ascension they are associated with
the disciples in the upper room (Acts i. 14).

According to a tradition, which we have no reason to
disbelieve, their conversion was due to the appearance of
the risen Lord to James, which is mentioned 1 Cor. xv. 7.

---

[1] Cf. i. 5, 6 and Mark xi. 23; i. 25 and John xiii. 17; ii. 5 and
Luke vi. 20; iv. 9 and Luke vi. 25; iv. 10 and Matt. xxiii. 12; v. 12
and Matt. v. 37.

Among the Christians at Jerusalem James soon took a prominent place, being, indeed, the recognised head of the Church there after the death of James, the brother of John (44 A.D.), and the dispersion of the other apostles. This commanding position he owed partly to the special relation in which he stood to Jesus, and partly to his own high character, which procured for him the name of the *Just* (or *Righteous*) and *Oblias* ("the bulwark of the people"). He is said to have been a Nazarite, and so much given to prayer in the Temple that his knees had grown hard like those of a camel. He was essentially a Hebrew of the Hebrews, who clung to the law and the prophets, and valued the Gospel as their fulfilment. Hence his name was sometimes used by the Judaising party in opposition to Paul (Gal. ii. 12 ; cf. Acts xv. 24)— as indeed it continued to be long after his death [1]— although he himself recognised Paul as the apostle of the Gentiles, and did not insist on a full observance of the law by Gentile converts (Gal. ii. 9 ; Acts xv. 19-21, 25, 26). He died a death of martyrdom, stoned by the Jews—as Josephus and Hegesippus relate—shortly before the destruction of Jerusalem, for his testimony to Jesus as the Messiah.

2. The Readers.—"To the twelve tribes which are of the Dispersion" (i. 1). In view of the Jewish traits in the epistle, which have been already pointed out, and having regard to the migratory habits of the readers (iv. 13), there is no reason to take these opening words in any other than a literal sense. Jews of the Dispersion were to be found in almost every part of the world, as appears from the narrative of the events which took place on the first Christian Pentecost (Acts ii. 5-11). The expression there used to describe the pilgrims who came up to Jerusalem, "devout men from every nation under

---

[1] In the (so-called) *Clementine Homilies* and *Recognitions.*

heaven," is supported by the evidence of many independent witnesses, such as Philo and Josephus. These exiled Jews were chiefly located in Babylon, Syria, and Egypt; and it was probably to those resident in Syria that copies of this epistle would be first sent. The epistle is addressed to Christian Jews (ii. 1, 7; v. 7, 8), of whom there were many in Syria liable to persecution and violence similar to that which Saul was inflicting on the Christians previous to his conversion; cf. ii. 6, 7 and Acts ix. 1, 2. While addressing himself mainly to Christian readers the writer seems also to have occasionally in view his unbelieving countrymen. The denunciations in v. 1-6 may be regarded as an apostrophe to the wealthy unbelievers, chiefly of the sect of the Sadducees, who truckled to the Romans and oppressed their poorer brethren, especially those who professed Christianity. James would have many opportunities of hearing of the trials which beset his believing countrymen in their distant homes; and, as he seems never to have left Jerusalem, it was natural that under a sense of the high responsibility attaching to his position he should wish to address them in writing as he does in this epistle.

3. Date and Place of Composition.—As both Scripture and tradition concur in representing James as having constantly resided at Jerusalem, there is no reason to doubt that the letter emanated from that city. With regard to the date of its composition there is less certainty. That it was written before the outbreak of the war, 66 A.D., which put an end to the Sadducean ascendency, is generally admitted. We may also infer, from the absence of any allusions to the sharp controversy regarding the obligations of the Jewish law on Gentile converts which gave rise to the Council of Jerusalem (50 A.D.), that it was either written before that event or not for some years afterwards.

On the whole, considering the marked absence from the epistle of anything like developed Christian doctrine, the continued expectation which it exhibits of Christ's speedy coming to judge the world (v. 8), and the application of the term Synagogue to an assembly of Christian worshippers (ii. 2), we are justified in assigning to the epistle a very early date—say 44-49 A.D. If this supposition be correct, we have here the oldest book of the New Testament.

4. Character and Contents.—This epistle is less doctrinal or theological than any other in the New Testament. It partakes largely of the ethical character of the Sermon on the Mount, which it resembles, not only in its general tone and sentiment, but in many of its expressions.[1] Its tone is eminently practical, the object of the writer being to inculcate Christian morality as essential to salvation (*e.g.* ii. 14-26). But it gives a prominent place to faith and patience (*e.g.* i. 2-12), and includes in its good works the careful ruling of the tongue (iii. 1-12). It also dwells much on the wisdom[2] which should characterise the religious man (*e.g.* iii. 13-18), and refers in detail to many other forms of duty—Christian practice being to the writer the highest form of outward worship (i. 27). The style of the epistle is sententious and forcible, passing swiftly, and sometimes without any apparent logical connection, from one topic to another, and it has about it not a little of the vehemence and fervour of the old prophets. James does not hesitate to denounce in very strong and plain terms, which savour,

---

[1] Cf. i. 2 and Matt. v. 10-12; i. 4 and Matt. v. 48; i. 5 and Matt. vii. 7-12; i. 20 and Matt. v. 22; ii. 13 and Matt. vi. 14, 15; ii. 14 and Matt. vii. 21-23; iv. 4 and Matt. vi. 24; iv. 10 and Matt. v. 3, 4; iv. 11 and Matt. vii. 1-5; v. 2 and Matt. vi. 19; v. 10 and Matt. v. 12; v. 12 and Matt. v. 34-37.

[2] Hence James has been called "the Apostle of Wisdom"; and the designation given to him in the Greek liturgy is that of "James the Wise."

in some respects, of the language of Amos,[1] the greed and
cruelty of the rich, the servility of the poor, and the
general vanity, strife, hypocrisy, and worldly-mindedness
which were characteristic of the Jews at this period of
their history, and had begun to infect the Christians in
their midst.

He insists on character as the test of true religion, and
demands that a man shall show the reality of his faith by
his life and conduct. In his protests against an empty
profession of religion, he is led into the use of language
which has sometimes been supposed (by Luther, for
example) to be irreconcilably at variance with the teaching of Paul.[2] But in reality there is no such inconsistency
between them.

The good works which James contends for are altogether different from the ritualistic observances which
Paul refused to acknowledge as necessary for salvation;
the justification he has in view in this epistle is not the
initial admission into the Divine favour which Paul's
Gentile converts needed, but the continuance of God's
people in a state of grace to which they are already
called; while the faith which he depreciates is not that
personal union with the Lord Jesus Christ which Paul
declared to be all-important for the Christian, but mere
intellectual belief, such as the acceptance of the mono-
theistic doctrine (ii. 19) that lay at the foundation of the
Jewish faith. No one can read Romans ii. 17-24 without
seeing that Paul would have concurred most heartily in
all that this epistle says about the necessity for carrying
religion into practice.

---

[1] Cf. iv. 13, v. 1, 2 and Amos viii. 5, 10; v. 5 and Amos vi. 1-6.

[2] It may have been the language of James ii. 10 that gave colour to
the misrepresentations referred to in Acts xv. 24.

CHAPTER XXI

1. Authorship.—There is abundant evidence to prove that this epistle was written by the apostle whose name it bears. Hardly any book of the New Testament is better supported by external evidence (extending as far back as the writings of Polycarp in the early part of the second century), while internally it bears in many of its features the stamp of Peter's mind, and the traces of his experience, as these are represented to us in the Gospels and in the Book of Acts.

From these sources we learn that the apostle was originally called "Simon, the son of John," and that he was a fisherman of Bethsaida before he attached himself to Jesus. With his brother Andrew, who brought him to Jesus, he was a disciple of John the Baptist before finding the Messiah. At His very first interview with the new disciple, Jesus discerned his great capacity for rendering service to His cause, and gave him a prophetic token of the part he was to play in the early history of His Church by conferring on him the new name of *Cephas* (in Greek, *Peter*, meaning rock or stone), (John i. 40-42). The significance of the name was more fully unfolded at a later time on the occasion of Peter's great confession of Jesus as the Christ (Matt. xvi. 13-19).

Like John and James, Peter was admitted to a closer
fellowship with his Master than the rest of the disciples
(Mark v. 37 ; Matt. xvii. 1 ; xxvi. 37, cf. Mark iii. 16, 17).
In company with John he was a witness of Christ's
trial in the high priest's palace, where he fell into the
threefold denial of his Master—to be bitterly repented of
immediately afterwards (Matt. xxvi. 69-75; Mark xiv.
66-72; Luke xxii. 54-62; John xviii. 15-27). On the
third day after the crucifixion the same disciples went
together early in the morning to the tomb and found it
empty, as Mary Magdalene had told them. The new
faith which then sprang up in Peter's heart was confirmed
by several interviews granted to him by the risen Christ,
who gave him a new commission, thrice uttered, to devote
himself to the interests of his Master's flock, and predicted that he would die a martyr's death (John xx. 1-10,
19; Luke xxiv. 33, 34; 1 Cor. xv. 5; John xxi.).

In the Book of Acts we find Peter acting as the leader
and spokesman of the early Church at several crises in its
history, viz. the election of an apostle in place of the
betrayer; the descent of the Holy Spirit on the day of
Pentecost; the admission of the Gentiles, in the person of
Cornelius, the Roman centurion, to the communion of the
Church; and the emancipation of the Gentile converts
from the bondage of the Jewish law at the Council of
Jerusalem, 50 A.D. (Acts i. 15-26; ii. 1-42; x.; xv.
6-11). It appears that some time afterwards Peter was
guilty of vacillation in his relations with Gentile Christians at Antioch—reminding us of his earlier weakness,—
which called forth a public remonstrance from the apostle
of the Gentiles (Gal. ii. 11-14).

Regarding Peter's subsequent life scarcely any information is furnished by the New Testament; but there
is an ancient and general tradition that he suffered
martyrdom at Rome. Many legends have gathered

round his imprisonment, death, and burial. The lack
of evidence for these need not prevent us from acqui-
escing in the general belief of the early Church that it
was at Rome Peter suffered the death by martyrdom
which had been predicted by his Lord. This is contra-
dicted by no other ancient tradition of the Church, and
we have some confirmation of it in this epistle (see p. 167).

In illustration of the remark already made as to the
harmony of this epistle with Peter's experience and
character, we may note the following points. (1) The
writer claims to have been "a witness of the sufferings
of Christ" (v. 1), and retains a vivid impression of them,
as shown in his description of Christ's patience (ii. 20-24)
and the frequency of his allusions to the subject. (2)
He gives prominence to Christ's resurrection, and represents it as the source of a new and living hope (i. 3, 4, 21 ;
iii. 20, 21), which had been precisely Peter's experience.
(3) He dwells upon the pastoral aspect of Christ's
ministry (ii. 25 ; v. 2-4) as if under an abiding sense of
the responsibility laid upon him by his Master's threefold
charge to act the part of a shepherd to His flock. (4)
He enlarges on the idea embodied in Peter's name, representing the Church as "a spiritual house" composed
of living stones, with Christ Himself as the chief corner-
stone (ii. 4-8)—an idea to which he had already given
expression in his address to the Sanhedrim (Acts iv. 11, 12),
after the example of his Lord—both quoting from the
Old Testament (Matt. xxi. 42). (5) His injunction to
his readers, "all of you gird yourselves with humility"
(literally, "put on humility like a slave's apron," v. 5),
sounds like a reminiscence of the Saviour's action which
so astonished Peter when "he took a towel and girded
himself" in order to wash His disciples' feet, saying, when
He had finished, "I have given you an example that ye
also should do as I have done to you" (John xiii. 2-17).

(6) His language in i. 17 ("And if ye call on him as Father, who without respect of persons," etc.) bears a strong resemblance to Peter's words at Cæsarea, "Of a truth I perceive that God is no respecter of persons," etc. (Acts x. 34). (7) In ii. 13-16, "Be subject to every ordinance of man for the Lord's sake . . . as free," we have probably the reproduction of the lesson taught to Peter by his Lord with regard to the payment of the tribute money (Matt. xvii. 24-27).

In the last-mentioned passage, as in many others, we can discern traces of the same graphic and pictorial style as we have seen to be characteristic of the Gospel of Mark, which, there is reason to believe, is largely a record of Peter's preaching. Such are the expressions, "not using your freedom for a cloke of wickedness" (ii. 16), the word translated "cloke" being peculiar to Peter (only used here), and meaning a *veil* or *covering;* "ye should put to silence the ignorance of foolish men" (ii. 15), the word rendered "put to silence" meaning, in a literal sense, to *muzzle* (as a dog), and being only applied elsewhere in the New Testament to the subduing of an unclean spirit, and the stilling of the raging sea—both in the Gospel of Mark (i. 25; iv. 39); "leaving you an example that ye should follow his steps" (ii. 21), the literal meaning of the word translated "example" being the *copy-head* set before a scholar for his patient and persevering imitation; "your adversary the devil, as a *roaring lion*, walketh about seeking whom he may devour" (v. 8). Akin to the pictorial style of the epistle is the "wealth of epithets" by which it is distinguished, *e.g.* "an inheritance incorruptible, and undefiled, and that fadeth not away" (i. 4). Cf. i. 7, 19; ii. 9, etc.

It appears from v. 12 that in writing this epistle Peter had the assistance of "Silvanus, our faithful brother," as his amanuensis, who is, no doubt, to be identified with the "Silas" mentioned in Acts xv. 22, 32, 40, and the Silvanus of 1 Thess. i. 1; 2 Thess. i. 1; 2 Cor. i. 19.

2. The Readers.—"To the elect who are sojourners of the Dispersion in Pontus, Galatia, Cappadocia, Asia, and Bithynia." The meaning of this address has been much disputed. By some it has been taken in a literal sense as denoting the Christian Jews of the Dispersion residing in the various parts of Asia Minor that are here specified. But this is inconsistent with the language used by the apostle to his readers in i. 14; ii. 9, 10 (where he quotes the same passage from Hosea that Paul applies to the calling of the Gentiles in Rom. ix. 25); iii. 6 (R.V.); iv. 3 (R.V.). All these passages would lead us to suppose that the readers of the epistle were largely Gentiles, as we know the members of the Churches in Asia Minor for the most part were.[1]

The words "sojourners of the Dispersion" are probably to be interpreted in a spiritual sense with reference to the heavenly Canaan, from which Christ's followers on earth may be regarded as temporary exiles, the Churches to which they belong being scattered branches of a commonwealth that has its home and its metropolis in heaven. This interpretation is justified by the whole tone of the epistle, which gives a spiritual meaning to the blessings of the Old Covenant.[2] It accords in particular with ii. 11, "Beloved, I beseech you as sojourners and pilgrims, to abstain from fleshly lusts, which war against the soul."

3. Date and Place of Composition.—The only thing

---

[1] For information regarding the Church in Pontus see Acts ii. 9; xviii. 2; in Galatia, pp. 87-94; in Cappadocia, Acts ii. 9; in Asia, Acts xviii. 24-26; xx. 17-35; Ephesians and Colossians. These Churches had received the Gospel from Paul and his associates. Hence the value of Peter's testimony in v. 12.

[2] In accordance with this is the view which regards Paul as the apostle of Gentile Christianity, James as the apostle of Jewish Christianity, Peter as holding an intermediate position between the two, and John as the apostle of universal Christianity.

we have to guide us as to the place of writing is in one of the closing salutations: "She that is in Babylon, elect together with you, saluteth you" (v. 13). Some suppose Peter's wife (1 Cor. ix. 5; Matt. viii. 14) to be here alluded to, but it is better to understand the Church in Rome, which city is here called "Babylon," as the new seat of oppression and cruelty to God's people. This was the view generally held by the early Church Fathers; it is in accordance with the figurative language of the epistle, referred to in the previous section; and it accounts for the strong resemblance between this epistle and that of Paul to the Romans, with which Peter could scarcely have failed to become acquainted during his residence in the capital.[1] It is almost certain that Babylon has this meaning in the Revelation; and it would add to the force of Peter's exhortations to courage and patience, that he was himself, when he wrote, in the very thick of the conflict.[2]

With regard to the date of its composition, the probability seems to be that the letter was written shortly after the outbreak of the Neronian persecution, when the Churches in the provinces were beginning to experience the effects of the imperial example at Rome, about 64-65 A.D.[3]

---

[1] *E.g.* cf. ii. 6-8, Rom. ix. 33, and Isa. viii. 14, xxviii. 16; ii. 13, 14, Rom. xiii. 1-4. A resemblance can also be traced to Ephesians and the Epistle of James, showing how little truth there is in Baur's theory of an irreconcilable opposition between Paul and the rest of the apostles (Salmon's *Introduction to the New Testament*, pp. 485-489).

[2] "That this epistle was written from Rome, I cannot doubt. It is impregnated with Roman thought to a degree beyond any other book in the Bible; the relation to the state and its officers forms an unusually large part of the whole" (Prof. Ramsay).

[3] The readers are addressed as liable to persecution, both of a social and a legal character, the very name of Christian having become a term of reproach, and still worse evils being imminent. Indeed, the signs of persecution are so pronounced in this epistle, that it has, on this account, been assigned by many to a later date.

4. Character and Contents.—This epistle breathes the spirit of practical earnestness so characteristic of its author. The Greek word "to do good" occurs no less than nine times in the course of the five chapters. There is no want of allusion to Christian privilege and Christian doctrine; but it is always for a practical purpose, as furnishing motives for Christian obedience. Of this we have an illustration in the frequent use of the words "wherefore," "therefore," "because," etc., by way of enforcing practical applications (i. 13, 16, 22; ii. 1, etc.). The chief duty which the writer wishes to inculcate is that of patience under trial (i. 6, 7; ii. 19-21; iii. 13-18; iv. 12-19). In many cases the suffering arose from persecution—proceeding from suspicion and ill-will on the part of the non-Christian members of the community (ii. 18, 19; iii. 16). The very name of Christian was becoming a term of reproach (iv. 16); and even worse trials were in store for them (iv. 12, 17). For the endurance of all such unmerited sufferings the apostle points them to the example of the Saviour (whose sufferings are referred to in every chapter), at the same time bidding them take care that they do not bring trouble on themselves by their unworthy conduct. Their trials, he reminds them, are only for a time (i. 6; iv. 7; v. 10), and will receive abundant compensation at the revelation of Christ's glory (i. 7; iv. 13, 14; v. 10). "The sufferings of Christ and the glories that should follow" are indeed the two poles around which the whole argument of the epistle turns, resulting in a beautiful blending of patience and hope. Hence Peter has been styled "the Apostle of Hope."[1]

Along with the calls to patience there are mingled various other admonitions addressed to citizens, ii. 13-17; servants, ii. 18-20; wives, iii. 1-6; husbands, iii. 7; elders

[1] As compared with John the apostle of love, Paul the apostle of faith, and James the apostle of works.

of the Church, v. 1-4; and the congregation generally,
with reference to various duties, iv. 5-11, etc. It is
worthy of note, that although this epistle has so little of
a speculative character, it has been the means of reveal-
ing two interesting truths, which would not have been
otherwise known to us (i. 12, last clause; iii. 18-20). It
may also be said to contain a practical refutation of the
Romish theory as to Peter's jurisdiction in the Church.
So far from making any claim to authority or pre-
eminence, the writer expressly puts himself on a level
with the other presbyters, and deprecates anything like a
spirit of lordship in the exercise of their ministry (v. 1-3).
The names "priest," "bishop," "Church," are never even
mentioned by him.[1]

[1] Except "Bishop" in ii. 25, where, however, it is Christ Himself
who is so designated.

CHAPTER XXII

2 PETER—JUDE [1]

"THE SECOND EPISTLE GENERAL OF PETER"

1. Authorship.—The genuineness of this epistle has been more questioned than that of any other book in the New Testament.[2] The external evidence for it is comparatively meagre. We seem to hear echoes of its language in some of the earliest post-apostolic works, but the first writer to make express and unmistakable mention of it is Origen (230 A.D.), and he does so in such a manner as to show that he has doubts about its genuineness. A century later it is classed by Eusebius among the disputed books of the New Testament.

The difficulty of accepting it as a genuine writing of Peter has chiefly arisen, both in ancient and in modern times, from its differing so greatly in tone and substance from the first epistle, written, as we have seen, near the close of Peter's life. There is scarcely any reference in

---

[1] On the connection between these two epistles, see p. 176.

[2] The question of genuineness really carries with it that of canonicity, as the epistle is written throughout in the name and with the authority of the Apostle Peter, and would lose its title to a place in the New Testament if it could be proved to be a forgery. Professor Ramsay would attribute it to "a disciple, who was full of the spirit and words of his teacher, and who believed so thoroughly that he was giving the views of his teacher, that he attributed it to that teacher."

it to our Saviour's sufferings or resurrection, which figure
so largely in the first epistle ; and what it chiefly inculcates is knowledge rather than hope.

But, apart from the versatility of Peter's mind, this
difference in the character of the two epistles may to a
large extent be accounted for by the different circumstances under which they were written. While the first
epistle was evidently designed to encourage and support
Christians under persecution, this later one was intended
to warn them against false teachers who were spreading
corruption in the Church. At the same time this epistle,
like the first, is eminently practical, insisting on the
necessity of Christian duty for the perfecting of Christian
knowledge, emphasising the danger of knowledge without
practice (i. 5-10 ; ii. 20, 21), and giving a practical turn to
the argument (iii. 11, 14). Moreover, amid the general
difference of style a close examination of the language and
thought in this epistle brings out many points of resemblance between it and Peter's language elsewhere. A likeness to the first epistle will be found on a comparison of the
undernoted passages.[1] It may also be seen in the frequent
use of twofold expressions, *e.g.* (in this epistle) "precious
and exceeding great," "not idle nor unfruitful," "without
spot and blameless" (i. 4, 8, 9, 19 ; ii. 3, 10, 13, etc.), and
in the marked recurrence in both epistles of the word
"holy." A number of verbal coincidences have also
been observed between this epistle and the Gospel of
Mark as well as between it and Peter's speeches in the
Book of Acts ; but they are for the most part of such
a nature as can only be appreciated by a student of the
original.[2]

---

[1] i. 2, 1 Pet. i. 2 ; i. 7, 1 Pet. i. 22, iii. 8 ; i. 19, 20, 1 Pet. i. 10-12;
ii. 1, 1 Pet. i. 18 ; iii. 5, 1 Pet. iii. 20 ; i. 3, 1 Pet. v. 10 ; iii. 14,
1 Pet. i. 19.

[2] Traced by Dr. Lumby in *Speaker's Commentary*, and *Expositor*,
vol. iv.. First Series.

It has also been found that this epistle, like the first, is distinguished by the use of rare words, of a striking and pictorial character, after the manner of Peter, but not borrowed from the first: *e.g.* "whose sentence now from of old *lingereth not*" (ii. 3), "*turning* the cities of Sodom and Gomorrah *into ashes*" (ii. 6), "*enticing* unstedfast souls," "they *entice* in the lusts of the flesh" (ii. 14, 18) (the word translated "entice" meaning literally to *take with a bait*, being such a word as a fisherman would naturally use) "which the ignorant and unstedfast *wrest*, as they do also the other scriptures" (iii. 16)— the Greek word for "wrest" meaning to *put on the rack*, like a criminal, for the purpose of extorting a desired confession.

It is worthy of remark as a note of genuineness that although the writer was evidently acquainted with the first epistle (iii. 1) he does not copy its designation of the apostle, as a forger might surely have been expected to do, nor does he attach the same address to the epistle, nor conclude with the same doxology (i. 1, 1 Pet. i. 1). Similarly, when he mentions the words spoken by the voice from heaven at the Transfiguration, he does not give them exactly as they are reported in the Gospels; and, in immediate connection with the Transfiguration, he makes use of two words, namely "tabernacle" and "decease," that would naturally be associated in Peter's mind with the memory of that great incident (i. 14-18, cf. Luke ix. 31-33). In his use of the expression in the same passage, "even as our Lord Jesus Christ signified unto me," we may trace an allusion to our Lord's prophecy of Peter's death in John xxi. 18, 19.[1]

---

[1] In the recurrence of the word "stablish," under a variety of forms, we have probably an illustration of the same retrospective tendency, which may be discerned also in the first epistle,—the reference, in this case, being to his Lord's injunction: "when once thou hast turned again, stablish thy brethren."

2. The Readers.—This epistle bears to be addressed to the same readers as the first (see p. 166).

3. Date and Place of Composition. — There is a strong probability that it was written before the destruction of Jerusalem. Otherwise such an impressive instance of divine judgment could scarcely have been left unnoticed in alluding to the retributive justice of God.

At the same time the errors and dangers described in this epistle, which bear a strong resemblance, in some respects, to those referred to in the pastoral epistles (1 Tim. iv. 1, 2; vi. 5, 20, 21; 2 Tim. ii. 18; iii. 1-7), prove that it could not have been written much sooner than 70 A.D. The allusion to Paul's epistles as known to the readers (iii. 15, 16) leads to the same conclusion, as does also the frequency of the expression "put in remembrance" and kindred words (i. 12, 13, 15; iii. 1, 2), which indicate an advanced period in the apostolic age, as well as in the life of Peter—assuming that he was the writer.

Like the first epistle, this was probably written from Rome; but the use of the apostle's Hebrew name of Symeon, or Simon (i. 1), as well as the connection of this epistle with that of Jude, would seem to indicate a Palestinian influence of some sort, possibly in the person of Peter's amanuensis or secretary.

4. Character and Contents.—This epistle, unlike the first, is full of denunciation and warning. It was designed to put its readers on their guard against false teachers, who were enticing unsteadfast souls, "promising them liberty while they themselves are bondservants of corruption." In opposition to their immoral doctrines it inculcates a steady and persevering endeavour after holiness as the only way to advance in true knowledge and secure an entrance into the eternal kingdom of our Lord and

Saviour Jesus Christ.   In particular, the writer seeks to
confute the arguments and counteract the influence of
certain scoffers who made light of the Second Coming,
as if it were a vain delusion, and appealed to the constancy of Nature as a warrant for their unbelief.   The
delay of the divine judgment the writer attributes to the
fact that "one day is with the Lord as a thousand years,
and a thousand years as one day," alleging the delay
to be a proof of God's mercy and long-suffering.   The
destruction of the world in the days of Noah is cited as
an act of divine judgment analogous to that which is to
take place at the end of the world, when the destroying
element, however, shall be not water but fire.   From the
dread catastrophe there shall arise " new heavens and a
new earth wherein dwelleth righteousness," for which
Christians ought to be preparing ; and the epistle concludes much in the same way as it commenced, with a
call to "grow in the grace and knowledge of our Lord
and Saviour Jesus Christ."

The intrinsic worth of the epistle is well expressed by
Calvin when he says, " the majesty of the Spirit of Christ
exhibits itself in every part of the epistle."

"THE GENERAL EPISTLE OF JUDE "

1. **Authorship.**—"Judas, a servant of Jesus Christ,
and brother of James."   It may be regarded as certain
that the James whom the writer here claims as his
brother was the well-known head of the Church at
Jerusalem, one of our Lord's brethren, and the writer of
the epistle that bears his name (cf. Matt. xiii. 55 ; Mark
vi. 3).   Jude is therefore not to be identified with any
of the apostles of the same name mentioned in the Gospels.
Had he been an apostle he would doubtless have claimed

the title, instead of being content to call himself "the brother of James." Regarding Jude personally we know little or nothing, but an interesting tradition concerning two of his grandsons has been preserved by Hegesippus. That historian (as quoted by Eusebius) tells how the Emperor Domitian, being moved with jealousy, sent for these two kinsmen of our Lord to inquire of them regarding the kingdom to which they aspired. When he learned from them that they were merely peasant proprietors farming a few acres of land in Palestine, and saw their hands horny with constant labour, and when they told him further that the kingdom to which they looked forward was not of this world, but to be revealed when Christ came to judge the quick and the dead, his alarm was removed, and he allowed them to depart in peace. Tradition tells that they lived to the reign of Trajan, honoured by the Church for their confession and for their relation to the Lord.

The obscurity of Jude himself is a strong argument for the genuineness of the epistle, as a forger would have chosen some more distinguished name to associate with his work. Its marked individuality also, exhibiting so many unusual features, by which it is distinguished from all the other books of the New Testament, except 2 Peter, is against the supposition of forgery. Although it is reckoned by Eusebius among the "disputed" books, we find it expressly quoted by Clement of Alexandria in the end of the second century, and recognised as canonical by Tertullian a few years later. It has also a place in the Muratorian Canon ; but it is absent from the Syriac Version.

2. **The Readers.**—On this subject we are left to conjecture. Considering the Jewish features of the book and the Jewish character of its author, it would seem probable that it was written to Christians in Palestine,

but not to any particular Church, as it contains no special salutations or messages.[1]

3. Date and Place of Composition.—Regarding the place of writing we have no direct information, but all the circumstances point to Palestine as the source of the epistle. From the absence of any allusion to the destruction of Jerusalem we infer it was written prior to that event; but here, as in 2 Peter, the evils with which the epistle deals preclude us from giving it a much earlier date. As an approximation we may name 65-68 A.D.

4. Character and Contents.—This epistle, consisting of a single chapter, bears a very striking likeness to the second chapter of 2 Peter, so much so that we may conclude with confidence that the one was borrowed from the other. As this epistle has certain features of originality about it which the other lacks, we may infer that St. Peter and not Jude was the borrower. It is quite possible, however, that the Epistle of Jude may itself be the translation of an Aramaic original—judging, for example, from its fondness for threefold expressions.[2]

The epistle is remarkable for several allusions to matters of ancient history that are not recorded in the Old Testament. In ver. 14 we have a quotation from an apocryphal book of Enoch (of which several copies of an Ethiopic version were brought from Abyssinia by the traveller Bruce in 1773, while a large part of it in Greek has been recently discovered in Egypt); and ver. 9 seems to have been derived from a book called "The Assumption of Moses," only a small part of which has been preserved to us. These allusions are not more at variance with the doctrine of Inspiration than the quotations in the

---

[1] The designation which the writer gives himself—Judas, the "*brother of James*"—was well fitted to command the attention of Jewish converts owing to the deep reverence in which James was held by his countrymen.

[2] Cf. vv. 1, 8, 11.

Old Testament from the "Book of Jasher," and other
such documents, or Paul's allusions to "Jannes and
Jambres" (2 Tim. iii. 8), or his quotations from heathen
writers. In 2 Peter, however, these quotations almost
disappear, and there is also an omission of one or two
references to Levitical uncleanness, as if the writer desired
to adapt his epistle as far as possible for general use.

The epistle is full of sharp and stern denunciation,
aimed at practical evils of a most heinous character,
committed by men who were "turning the grace of our
God into lasciviousness, and denying our only Master and
Lord, Jesus Christ." These evils were founded upon a
gross abuse of Christian liberty, and were somewhat
similar to the terrible excesses which broke out among
the Anabaptists after the Protestant Reformation, resulting from the abuse of the doctrine of Justification
by Faith, when professing Christians combined the guilt
of Cain (bloodshed), of Balaam (seduction), and of Korah
(insubordination), ver. 11. In view of the corruption
both of faith and manners that was thus beginning to
infect the Church, Jude exhorts his readers to "contend
earnestly for the faith which was once for all delivered
unto the saints," and appeals to the past history of God's
judgments for proof of the punishment in store for the
present offenders, whom he commends nevertheless to the
compassion and care of their believing brethren.

The epistle concludes with one of the most beautiful
doxologies to be found in the New Testament.

CHAPTER XXIII

1, 2, AND 3 JOHN

"THE FIRST EPISTLE GENERAL OF JOHN"

1. Authorship.—This epistle was used by two of the Fathers who had been disciples of the Apostle John, viz. Polycarp and Papias. It was recognised and quoted as John's by Irenæus who had been a disciple of Polycarp, and it was evidently known by the writer of the *Letter to Diognetus*. It is freely quoted by Clement of Alexandria and Tertullian, is referred to in the Muratorian Fragment, and is one of the books contained in the Syriac as well as in the old Latin Version.

Its internal character is such as to confirm us in the belief that it was written by the author of the fourth Gospel. Not only has it many verbal similarities,[1] but it is dominated by the same Christian idealism which refers all things in human life to the ultimate principles of light and darkness, truth and error, good and evil, love and hatred, life and death, God and the devil. So intimate is the connection between the two books that

---

[1] *E.g.* cf. i. 1, John i. 1, 14, xx. 27 ; i. 2, John iii. 11 ; i. 3, John xvii. 21 ; i. 4, John xvi. 24 ; i. 5, 6, John i. 5, iii. 21, viii. 12 ; ii. 11, John xii. 35 ; iii. 14, John v. 24 ; iv. 9, John i. 14, iii. 16 ; iv. 14, John iv. 42 ; v. 6, John xix. 34.

the epistle was regarded by the late Bishop Lightfoot
and others as forming a postscript to the Gospel.[1]

2. The Readers.—In all probability it was addressed
in the first instance to the Churches of Asia, among
whom the Apostle John spent the latter part of his life.
The exhortation in v. 21, "guard yourselves from idols,"
would have special significance in the neighbourhood of
Ephesus, which was a great stronghold of idolatry; and the
absence of allusions to the Old Testament bears out the
supposition that the epistle was addressed to converts
from heathenism. Although there is no salutation either
at the beginning or the end, and no personal or historical
allusions such as would have been likely to occur if it
had been a letter addressed to an individual Church, yet
the writer speaks in a quiet tone of authority as if he
were well known to his readers and expected that his
words would command respect. He addresses them in
terms of affection, and writes as if he were well acquainted
with their dangers and their needs.[2]

3. Date and Place of Composition.—It was probably
written in the same city as tradition assigns to the
Gospel, viz. Ephesus; and about the same time—85-90
A.D. It takes the Gospel for granted, and in certain
passages (*e.g.* ii. 1, etc., "my little children") the tone of
its language is such as would befit an aged apostle
addressing men of a later generation.

4. Character and Contents.—In this epistle—probably
the last inspired utterance of the New Testament except-
ing the two brief missives that follow it—we have the

---

[1] Professor Ramsay says : "No two works in the whole range of
literature show clearer signs of the genius of one writer."

[2] Augustine and other Latin writers speak of the epistle as
addressed *to the Parthians,* but this was probably a mistake occasioned by the Greek term *parthenos* ("virgin"), which was frequently
applied to the Apostle John, in allusion to his supposed lifelong
celibacy.

translation into the Christian life of those great truths, regarding the fellowship of God with man, that are found in the fourth Gospel in connection with the life and ministry of Jesus Christ. That Gospel, as we have seen, is doctrinal as well as historical, but its doctrines are here applied to the lives of Christ's followers. The epistle is thus in advance of the Gospel, being designed to lead Christians to a conscious realisation of the new life to which they are called in fellowship with Christ—a life transcending and vanquishing that of the world (cf. v. 4, 5, 12, 13, and i. 4 with John xx. 31).

Its thought springs mainly out of a twofold conception of the Divine Nature as "light" (i.-ii.), and as "love" (iv. 7–v.), united by a bond of righteousness (ii. 29–iv. 6). There is no laboured argument such as we find in some of Paul's epistles, but simply an appeal to first principles that are to be seen with the spiritual eye, not to be proved by means of logic.

Although lofty and spiritual, the teaching in the epistle is at the same time intensely practical. It was evidently intended to counteract the growing tendency to magnify knowledge at the expense of practice (i. 6, 7 ; ii. 3-6 ; iii. 6-10 ; cf. ii. 18, 19). One form of this incipient Gnosticism was associated with the name of Cerinthus, who lived at Ephesus in the time of the apostle. Cerinthus, like many others,[1] denied the reality of Christ's humanity, maintaining, in particular, that the Divine Being only entered into the man Jesus at his Baptism and left him on the eve of his Passion. Hence the emphatic statement of the apostle (v. 6), "This is he that came by water and blood, even Jesus Christ; not with the water only, but with the water and with the blood," implying that the Saviour fulfilled His divine mission in His death upon the cross as well as in His

[1] Called *Docetæ* from a Greek word meaning *apparent*, not real.

baptism. Again and again, in other passages, the apostle insists on the reality of the union between Jesus and the Christ, as an essential element of the Christian faith (ii. 22 ; iv. 2, 3, 15 ; v. 1, 5 ; cf. i. 1-4).

While it gives no quarter to evil and falsehood, the epistle overflows with exhortations to the love of God and man (ii. 9-11 ; iii. 11-18 ; iv. 7-13, 16-21 ; v. 1, 2). As we read the apostle's language here, we find it easy to believe the story told of him by Jerome, that when he was too old to preach he used to be carried to church, simply to repeat in the hearing of the congregation, "Little children, love one another." And when some one asked him, "Master, why dost thou always speak thus ?" he answered, "Because it is the Lord's command ; and if only this be done, it is enough."

"THE SECOND EPISTLE OF JOHN"

1. Authorship. — The external evidence for the genuineness of this epistle is not so convincing as in the case of the one that we have just been considering ; but this is easily accounted for by its brevity and its being less suitable for public reading in church. At the same time, it is expressly quoted (as John's) by Irenæus and Clement of Alexandria, and is mentioned in the Muratorian Fragment. It appears also to have been acknowledged by Eusebius, although he placed it among the "disputed" books. With regard to internal evidence, it has all the appearance of being genuine. Like the third epistle it bears to be written by "the elder," a designation which implies that the writer was a well-known personage in the Church, and which might be fitly claimed by John as the last of the apostles.[1] But an

---

[1] Cf. Peter's use of the expression "a fellow-elder," as applied to himself (1 Peter v. 1), and the language of Papias (Appendix, p. 195).

imitator who wished to pass for John would have made
his claim in more distinct terms ; and the contents of the
epistle are such that no reasonable motive can be assigned
for forgery.

The genuineness of this epistle derives considerable
support also from its strong resemblance to the first,—
no less than seven of its thirteen verses having something parallel in the other.[1]

2. The Reader. — "Unto the elect lady and her
children." It is a question whether these words are to
be taken literally, or in a figurative sense as the designation of a Church and its members. On the whole the
latter seems the more probable, in view of the expressions
used in verses 1, 4, 5, 10, 13. Such figurative language
need not surprise us in the case of a writer so fond of
symbolism as the author of the Apocalypse and the fourth
Gospel.[2] But which of the Churches in Asia is thus
addressed we have no means of knowing.

3. Date and Place of Composition.—It was probably
written from Ephesus,—subsequently to the first epistle.

4. Character and Contents.—While the epistle contains expressions of warm affection for the members of
the Church in question (whom the writer appears to have
recently visited), its main object is to warn them against
the insidious and corrupting influence of certain heretical
teachers who were going about denying the reality of
Christ's humanity (ver. 7). "The elder" urges an uncompromising opposition to all such teachers, in terms
that remind us of the story told of John by Irenæus on
the authority of those who had received it from Polycarp,

---

[1] Cf. ver. 1 and 1 John iii. 18 ; ver. 4 and iv. 21 ; ver. 5 and ii.
7 ; ver. 6 and v. 3 ; ver. 7 and iv. 1-3 ; ver. 9 and ii. 23 ; ver. 12
and i. 4.

[2] Some think that a similar metaphor is to be found in the First
Epistle of Peter (v. 13), whom tradition associates in his later years
with John.

that finding Cerinthus in a public bath, the apostle rushed out at the sight of him, exclaiming, "Let us fly lest even the bath fall on us, because Cerinthus, the enemy of the truth, is within,"—a speech that betrays a lingering of the spirit that had once been rebuked by his Lord (Luke ix. 54). On the other hand, the blending of love[1] with truth in the earlier part of the epistle is equally characteristic of the disciple "whom Jesus loved"; and it finds similar illustration in the beautiful story of "St. John and the Robber."[2]

"THE THIRD EPISTLE OF JOHN"

1. Authorship.—If we admit the second epistle to be the work of John, we can have no difficulty in accepting this also as his. The two epistles have been aptly termed "twins";[3] and the contents of this epistle are so peculiar in their bearing on the position and the authority of the writer, as to preclude the idea of forgery.

2. The Reader.—"Unto Gaius the beloved." - The name Gaius occurs several times in the New Testament;[4] but whether the receiver of this letter is to be identified with any of those who are elsewhere so called it is impossible to say, the name being a very common one. He

---

[1] The word "love" (noun or verb) occurs six times in this short epistle, and "truth" five times.

[2] The story is told by Eusebius (iii. 33). The Apostle John had left in charge of the local bishop a promising young man who was duly baptized and instructed. On his return he surprised the bishop by asking for his "deposit," adding, in explanation of his words, "I demand the young man, the soul of a brother." Thereupon the bishop had to confess that the young man had gone astray and become a robber-chief. The apostle immediately called for a horse and made his way to the haunts of the robber, who fled at his approach. The apostle pursued and overtook him, and by his persuasions and tears induced him to give up his evil life and return to his old home, to be restored to the Church.

[3] For resemblances cf. ver. 1 and 2 John ver. 1; ver. 3, 4 and 2 John ver. 4; ver. 13 and 2 John ver. 12.

[4] Acts xix. 29; xx. 4; Rom. xvi. 23; 1 Cor. i. 14.

is addressed as a faithful and liberal member of the Church (verses 1-6).

3. Date and Place of Composition.—Like the second, this epistle was probably written from Ephesus,—subsequently to the first.

4. Character and Contents.—This epistle, like the second, gives us a momentary glimpse of Church-life in Asia towards the close of the first century. While the second contains a warning against heresy, this relates rather to the evil of schism. It shows us the practical difficulties which had to be encountered in the government of the Church. In Gaius (the recipient of the letter) we have a sincere and charitable Christian whose influence and example the writer invokes in opposition to the factious and intolerant conduct of an ambitious ecclesiastic named Diotrephes, who had gone so far as to close his doors on "the brethren" who had come in the name of "the elder," apparently bearing a letter from him—perhaps our second epistle (verses 9, 10). The aged head of the Church feels that it will be necessary, the next time he visits the district, to hold a reckoning with the offender for his malice and presumption.[1] Meanwhile he warns Gaius against being led astray by the example of Diotrephes; and in pleasing contrast with the latter he refers to one Demetrius—apparently the bearer of this letter—who "hath the witness of all men, and of the truth itself." Finally he pleads the same excuse for his brevity as he does in the case of the second epistle, viz. that he hopes soon to visit his readers, when they "shall speak face to face."

---

[1] "The calm confidence of St. John seems to rest on himself more than on his official power. His presence will vindicate his authority. The growth of the Churches is as plainly marked as their independence. The first place in them has become an object of unworthy ambition. They are able, and as it appears, for the most part willing to maintain missionary teachers." (Westcott.)

CHAPTER XXIV

1. Authorship.—There is very strong external evidence to prove that this book was written by the Apostle John. Passing over some earlier apparent witnesses, we find unmistakable mention of it in the writings of Justin Martyr. He expressly refers to it as the work of the apostle, in the dialogue which he held with Trypho, an unbelieving Jew, in the very city of Ephesus where John lived, and within half a century after his death. Equally clear and explicit is the testimony of Irenæus, who, as we have seen, was a disciple of Polycarp, the disciple of John. In one passage Irenæus even gives as his authority for preferring 666 to 616 as "the number of the beast," in the disputed reading (xiii. 18), the testimony of those who had seen John face to face. The book is twice mentioned in the Canon of the Muratorian Fragment, once in such a way as to imply that it was publicly read in church; it was one of the books on which Melito, Bishop of Sardis, wrote a commentary (about 170 A.D.); and it is expressly quoted as "the Scripture" in the letter sent by the persecuted Christians of Vienne and Lyons to their brethren in Asia Minor (177 A.D.).

But soon after the middle of the second century the

book began to be regarded with suspicion, owing to the use made of it by a heretical party called the Montanists, who indulged in extravagant notions regarding the "thousand years" of Christ's reign with His saints which was to take place before the end of the world (xx.). This feeling of distrust was strengthened by observing what a marked difference there was in the language and style of the Revelation as compared with the other works ascribed to John; and a considerable amount of controversy took place on the subject. Ultimately, however, the objections were overruled, and the book obtained general acceptance in the Church.

In modern times the controversy has been renewed; and objectors are still disposed to insist, as of old, on the internal marks of a different authorship from that of the fourth Gospel.[1]   In particular it is pointed out that whereas the Gospel is written in good Greek, the Revelation is full of grammatical mistakes and eccentricities; so that while there is scarcely anything in the former to show that the writer was other than a Greek, the latter would give us the impression of its having been written by a person who first thought in Hebrew and had afterwards to turn his thoughts into a language with which he was imperfectly acquainted.

To meet this objection the following considerations may be adduced :—

(1) The difference in the nature and contents of the two books; the one being mainly narrative or colloquial, the other being formed on the model of the Old Testament prophets.   (2) The possible effect on the apostle of many years' residence in Ephesus (if we accept the earlier date assigned to the Revelation) in the way of improving his knowledge of Greek.   (3) The unfavour-

---

[1] The Tübingen school, however, generally admit Revelation as the work of the apostle, and reject the fourth Gospel.

able circumstances under which he appears to have written the Revelation ; and the possible employment by him of a skilled Greek amanuensis in the composition of his Gospel.

On the other hand, amid all the diversity between the two books both in ideas and in language, there are not wanting some important features of resemblance, betokening an identity of authorship.

(1) The name "Lamb" is only applied to the Saviour in the fourth Gospel (i. 29, 36) and in the Revelation (v. 6, 8, 12, etc.), although it is indirectly referred to in 1 Peter i. 19 and Acts viii. 32. In like manner the name "Word" is only applied to the Saviour in the Gospel of John (i. 1, etc.), in First Epistle of John (i. 1, "the Word of life"), and in the Revelation (xix. 13, "The Word of God").

(2) Some of John's favourite expressions, such as, "he that overcometh," "witness" (noun or verb), "keep (my) word," are of frequent occurrence in the Revelation.

(3) In Revelation i. 7 we seem to hear an echo of John xix. 34-37, where alone the piercing of our Lord with the spear is recorded, and where there is the same quotation of Zech. xii. 10—in the same unusual form.

(4) The Greek word meaning "true" or "real," in opposition to what is false or counterfeit, occurs nine times in St. John's Gospel, four times in 1 John, and ten times in the Revelation; but only five times in all the rest of the New Testament.

(5) The Revelation, like the fourth Gospel, recognises our Lord's pre-eminence and His title to divine honours (i. 8, 17, 18 ; iii. 14, 21 ; v. 9, 13 ; xix. 16 ; xxii. 13).

(6) A still stronger feature of resemblance may be seen in the similarity of the representations which the two books give of the Saviour's triumph as resulting

from successive conflicts marked by apparent and temporary defeat.   In these conflicts the Gentiles, centred
in "Babylon," take the place held by the unbelieving
Jews in the Gospel ; and the "disciples" of the earlier days
are represented by the Church, or "the bride" (of
Christ).

It has been objected that the Revelation, unlike the
other writings of John, gives the name of its avowed
author (i. 1, 4, 9; xxii. 8).   But this is sufficiently
accounted for by the prophetical character of the book.
It was the practice of the prophets of the Old Testament, although not of the historians, to mention their
names in their writings.

2. The Readers.—It was evidently meant for the
Church at large—represented by "the seven Churches
which are in Asia" (i. 4).

3. Date and Place of Composition.—From i. 9 we
learn that the revelation was made to John when he
"was in the isle that is called Patmos" (in the Ægean
Sea) "for the word of God and the testimony of Jesus."
From i. 11; x. 4; xiv. 13; xix. 9; xxi. 5, we should
infer that it was committed to writing in the island
immediately after it was received.   As to the date of
the apostle's banishment to Patmos, Irenæus expressly
mentions that the vision was seen almost within his own
generation at the end of the reign of Domitian (Emperor
81-96 A.D.).   There is nothing in any earlier writer to
throw discredit on this statement ; and there are several
things in the book itself which seem to point to a late
date of composition, *e.g.* the important and intimate
relation in which John appears to stand to the principal
Churches of Asia Minor, the signs of marked spiritual
declension in several of these Churches (ii. 4, 5 ; iii. 1, 2),
the use of the expression "the Lord's day" (i. 10),
instead of the earlier "first day of the week," and of the

phrase "synagogue of Satan" (ii. 9 ; iii. 9), which would scarcely have been employed by a Christian writer previous to the destruction of Jerusalem.

At the same time there are some observations by writers later than Irenæus that favour an earlier date. Tertullian tells us that at Rome the Apostle John was plunged in burning oil, without sustaining any injury, and that he was afterwards banished to an island. It is in connection with the martyrdom of Peter and Paul that he makes the remark, which suggests the close of Nero's reign as the time referred to ; and accordingly we find Jerome (about the end of the fourth century) making an explicit statement to that effect. It is quite possible Irenæus may have made a mistake, occasioned perhaps by the frequency of banishment in the reign of Domitian ; and this is the view taken by some critics at the present day, who can only account for the style and character of the book on the supposition that it was written a considerable time before the Gospel. The key to the interpretation of the book, they conceive, is to be found in the identification of the reigning king in xvii. 10 with the Emperor Galba, the successor of Nero. The latter is regarded as the head of the beast referred to in xiii. 3, the healing of its wound symbolising the restoration of Nero, who was then supposed to be still alive and in hiding in the East. Confirmation of this is found in xvii. 8, 11, and also in the symbolical "number of the beast" ("the number of a man . . . Six hundred and sixty and six," xiii. 18), which answers in Hebrew letters to the name "Neron Cæsar." But it would be more natural to reckon the number in Greek letters (as Irenæus did) ; and in either case a correspondence to it can be made out in the case of a great many other prominent names. This weakens very much the force of the argument, for "we cannot infer much from the fact that a key fits the lock, if it is a lock in which almost any key will turn." [1]

4. Character and Contents. — The Revelation or *Apocalypse* (a Greek word meaning "uncovering") has many of the characteristics of the Book of Daniel. Both

[1] Whatever interpretation we may give to the "number of the beast," there is now a growing conviction that the theory which dates the composition of the book before the destruction of Jerusalem must be abandoned, and that the persecution referred to is not that which took place at Rome in the reign of Nero, but the sufferings inflicted on Christians at a later date, in the provinces, especially in Asia Minor, when they refused to worship the Emperor and Roma. In support of this conclusion the following considerations may be adduced. (1) "The absolute and irreconcilable opposition between the Church and the Empire" which distinguishes this book from all the other writings of the New Testament, even the latest of them. (2) The description of Rome as "the great harlot that sitteth upon many waters, with whom the kings of the earth committed fornication, . . . the woman drunken with the blood of the saints, and with the blood of the martyrs of Jesus,"—which finds its explanation in the fact that the worship of Roma had spread over the Empire, and was now the most formidable rival that Christianity had to contend with. (3) The reference to Pergamum as the place "where Satan's throne is, . . . where Satan dwelleth"—that city having been the first place in Asia to possess a temple in honour of the Emperor (*Augusteum*), and having been the scene of a Christian martyrdom, apparently many years before the Apocalypse was written, "even in the days of Antipas my witness, my faithful one, who was killed among you." (4) The nature of the death suffered by the martyrs : "and I saw the souls of them that had been beheaded for the testimony of Jesus, and for the word of God, and such as worshipped not the beast, neither his image, and received not the mark upon their forehead and upon their hand"—as beheading was a common form of punishment with proconsuls, but not in use at Rome during the Neronic persecution.

As to the precise date which, according to this view, is to be assigned to the composition of the book, there is room for difference of opinion. Mommsen argues for the later years of Vespasian (75-80 A.D.) chiefly on account of the interpretation which he gives to certain passages, as referring to the expectation of the later pseudo-Nero's return with the help of the Parthians. Apart from this there seems to be no good reason why we should not accept the statement of Irenæus, already referred to, that the Revelation came to John in the closing years of Domitian, whose name is traditionally associated with persecution of the Christians (of which we have some traces in the writings of Dion Cassius and Suetonius), and who took delight in the homage paid to him as emperor, and in the title of *dominus et deus* which had already been claimed by his predecessor Caligula.

books consist largely of prophecy couched in the language of symbolism.   This was a mode of expression frequently adopted by Jewish writers towards the close of the Old Testament dispensation, when, owing to foreign oppression, it would have been dangerous to speak plainly in matters affecting the national interests.

The central theme is the second coming of Christ, in a magnificent setting of imagery—designed to represent the great struggles and events that are to precede the final consummation.

"After the Prologue, which occupies the first eight verses, there follow seven sections—

1. The letters to the Seven Churches of Asia (i. 9–iii. 22).

2. The Seven Seals (iv.-vii.).

3. The Seven Trumpets (viii.-xi.).

4. The Seven Mystic Figures — The Sun - clothed Woman; the Red Dragon; the Man-child; the Wild Beast from the Sea; the Wild Beast from the Land; the Lamb on Mount Sion; the Son of Man on the Cloud (xii.-xiv.).

5. The Seven Vials (xv.-xvi.).

6. The Doom of the Foes of Christ (xvii.-xx.).

7. The Blessed Consummation (xxi.–xxii. 7).   The Epilogue (xxii. 8-21)." [1]

The unity of the book is one of its most striking features; and the attempts which have recently been made by some critics to assign it to several different authors have not been attended with success.

It must be acknowledged that the interpretation of the Revelation in detail is still, to a great extent, shrouded in mystery.   Even those who feel assured that Nero is the man represented by the number of "the beast," and that the prophecy was delivered before the complete

---

[1] Farrar's *Messages of the Books*, p. 520.

Destruction of Jerusalem, find themselves beset with insuperable difficulties when they come to deal with certain portions of the book, while in other passages their theory would seem to imply that some of the predictions of the Seer were very soon falsified by events. This is a supposition which it is almost as difficult to reconcile with the high estimation in which the Apocalypse continued to be held by the early Church, as with its divine inspiration.

The safest and probably the truest interpretation of the book is to regard it as a symbolic representation of great principles rather than as a collection of definite predictions. In other words, it is intended for the edification and comfort of Christ's people, not to give detailed information regarding the future to those who are clever enough to solve its enigmas. "Here, if anywhere, faith and love are the key to knowledge, not knowledge the key to faith and love. It is in the very spirit of the book, not in a spirit hard or narrow or unsympathetic, that it closes with the words ‘the grace of the Lord Jesus Christ be with the saints.’"[1]

[1] Dr. Milligan on the Book of Revelation.

APPENDIX A

THE first six of the following are usually called the "Apostolic Fathers" :—

Clement of Rome, according to an ancient and unanimous tradition, was one of the earliest bishops of the Roman Church. Among the numerous writings that have been ascribed to him, only one is now regarded as genuine, which is known as his 1st Epistle to the Corinthians. The letter is written in the name of the Roman Church, not without a tone of authority (although there is scarcely any more trace in it than in the New Testament of episcopal jurisdiction in a monarchical sense, the terms "bishop" and "presbyter" being still used as convertible). The object of the epistle was to cure the dissension and insubordination that had broken out in the Corinthian Church, and which had led to the deposition of some blameless presbyters. The date now generally assigned to the letter, on what appear to be adequate grounds, is 95-96 A.D. The 2nd Epistle of Clement, so called, is a homily by an unknown author, probably written at Rome in the first half of the second century.

Ignatius, converted to Christianity comparatively late in life, succeeded Euodius as Bishop of Antioch, and was martyred in the arena of the Coliseum at Rome, under Trajan, 110-115 A.D. His genuine writings are now generally held to consist of seven epistles, written in the course of his last journey, as a prisoner, from Antioch to Rome, viz. :— (from Smyrna) to the Ephesians, the Magnesians, the

Trallians, the Romans, and (from Troas) to the Philadelphians, the Smyrnæans, and Polycarp, Bishop of Smyrna. With the exception of the Epistle to the Romans, which relates almost entirely to the author's expected and eagerly-desired martyrdom, these epistles deal with questions of doctrine and discipline. They emphasise the reality of Christ's humanity in opposition to Docetic error (cf. p. 180), denounce Judaising tendencies, and enforce the threefold ecclesiastical order (bishop, presbyter, and deacon) in the interests of Church unity.

Polycarp, for many years Bishop of Smyrna, was born about 69-70 A.D., and suffered martyrdom in that city about 155-156 A.D., when he was in his eighty-sixth year. From his disciple, Irenæus, we learn that he had been a hearer of the Apostle John, and that he had "not only been taught by apostles, and lived in familiar intercourse with many that had seen Christ," but had also "received his appointment in Asia from Apostles as bishop in the Church of Smyrna." The only extant writing bearing his name that is generally admitted to be genuine is his epistle to the Philippians, which was written nearly forty-five years before his death, about the time of Ignatius' martyrdom. It is of considerable length, but does not display much originality, borrowing largely from the teaching of "the Lord" and His apostles, as well as from the letters of Ignatius and Clement; and the chief value of his writing, as of his life, consisted in his unswerving attachment, in an age of transition and conflict, to the genuine apostolic tradition.

Barnabas.—To this well-known associate of St. Paul there was ascribed by the early Church Fathers an epistle containing twenty chapters. It is very anti-Judaistic in spirit, maintaining that Judaism, in its outward and visible form, had not received the divine sanction, and that God's covenant had never belonged to the Jews. It betrays an imperfect acquaintance with Jewish rites and ceremonies, and a tendency to indulge in trifling allegories, for which reasons, as well as because of its Gnostic magnifying of the inner meaning of Scripture at the expense of its historical framework, most critics assign it to an unknown Gentile author of Alexandria, writing in the beginning of the second

century. But it contains allusions and arguments which
seem to imply that the destruction of the Temple had been
a recent occurrence ; and, for this and other reasons, some
would assign it to about 80 A.D., and accept the tradition
that it was the work of Barnabas.

The Shepherd of Hermas.—This is the name of a work
which was held in high esteem both by the Eastern and
Western Church for hundreds of years, from about the
middle of the second century. It bears to be written by one
Hermas, whom Origen, without any definite or sufficient
reason, identifies with the Hermas of Rom. xvi. 14. It
consists of three parts : (1) Visions seen by Hermas (in
Rome and the neighbourhood) ; (2) Commandments, and (3)
Similitudes which were delivered to Hermas by one who
appeared to him in the guise of a shepherd, "the angel of
repentance,"—the whole book being a call to repentance.
Internal evidence has led some to assign it to the latter part
of the first century ; but if we are to accept a statement regarding it in the Muratorian Canon, it would appear not to
have been composed till the middle of the second century.

Papias, Bishop of Hierapolis, published an *Exposition of
Oracles of the Lord* about 135 A.D. Only a few brief passages
of the work have been preserved for us (by Irenæus and
Eusebius), but Papias is frequently referred to by other
writers. Eusebius characterises him as "a man of very mean
capacity," though very learned ; and both he and Irenæus
refer to his peculiar views, of a materialistic nature, on the
subject of the Millennium. The chief object of his work
above-mentioned seems to have been to interpret the Gospels
in the light of all the traditions he could collect from the
Lord's disciples or those acquainted with them. According
to Irenæus, Papias was a hearer of the Apostle John, a companion of Polycarp, and a man of the olden time ; but
Eusebius inferred (rightly or wrongly) from his language
(which he quotes) that there were two persons of the name of
John, and that it was not John the Apostle, but John the
Elder, that Papias was acquainted with. The words of
Papias are as follows :—"If I met anywhere with any one
who had been a follower of the Elders, I used to enquire as
to the discourses of the Elders—what was said by Andrew,

or by Peter, or by Philip, or by Thomas or James, or by John or Matthew, or any other of the Lord's disciples, and what Aristion and the Elder John, the disciples of the Lord, say. For I did not think that I would get so much profit from the contents of books as from the utterances of a living and abiding voice." There is room for difference of opinion as to the correctness of this inference by Eusebius.

The *Didaché* or "**Teaching of the (Twelve) Apostles**" is the name of the work referred to by Eusebius and others —Clement of Alexandria even quoting it as "Scripture"; but no MS. of it was known till 1873, when Bryennius discovered at Constantinople a document containing both it and the epistles of Clement and Barnabas, and several other ancient writings. The first part of it is founded upon a still earlier work called "The Two Ways" (probably of Jewish origin, and perhaps also used in the epistle of Barnabas), which sets forth the way of righteousness and life, and the way of unrighteousness and death, somewhat after the manner of the Epistle of James. The second part is of a more ecclesiastical nature, and relates to prayer and fasting, the two sacraments, and various classes of teachers and office-bearers in the Church, concluding with an exhortation to watch and be ready for the second coming of the Lord. It was probably composed in the end of the first or the beginning of the second century.

Aristides, an Athenian philosopher, is mentioned by Eusebius and other writers as the author of a famous Apology. It is only within the last few years that the work has been discovered, in a Syriac translation, in St. Catherine's, Mount Sinai—which has led to the identification of a portion of the original, embodied in an early Christian romance (*The Life of Barlaam and Josaphat*). It was addressed to the Emperor Hadrian (117-138 A.D.), or to his successor, Antoninus Pius (who was also called Hadrian), or possibly to both, and it may safely be assigned to 125-140 A.D. It is the oldest extant Christian Apology. That of Quadratus, which was written about the same time, is still undiscovered; but a quotation from it is given by Eusebius, who speaks highly of the work.

Basilides, a famous Gnostic speculator, taught at Alexandria in the reign of Hadrian (117-138 A.D.). We learn from Eusebius that he wrote twenty-four books on the Gospel, and that a satisfactory refutation of his heresy was produced by Agrippa Castor. A considerable portion of his writings has been found in Hippolytus' *Refutation of all Heresies*, recovered in 1842 and published in 1851 ; and various accounts of his teaching are found in the writings of Clement of Alexandria, Irenæus, and Epiphanius. " He seems to have sought to embrace all the universe in one plan, of which Jesus Christ is the centre, and to have broken down in the attempt to combine Egyptian speculation with Scripture truth." Although his name is often mentioned by subsequent writers, he founded no school of importance, his only eminent disciple being his son Isidore.

Valentinus, another Gnostic, whose fame eclipsed that of Basilides, came to Rome (from the East) about 138 A.D., and taught there for about thirty years. From Irenæus, Hippolytus, and other ancient writers who discuss his views, we learn that he devised an elaborate system of *Aeons* or emanations from the Deity, forming the *Pleroma* or universe, for which he professed to find support in the New Testament, although he was in reality more of a Pythagorean than a Christian.

Marcion, the son of a Bishop of Sinope in Pontus, but excommunicated on account of his heresy, became a Gnostic leader of great influence at Rome and elsewhere (about 140 A.D.), with followers in many lands not only in his own day but for generations afterwards. He set the New Testament in opposition to the Old, and represented the God of Redemption as essentially different from and superior to the God of Creation. To suit his purposes he framed a Gospel for himself, being a mutilated Gospel of Luke ; and of the rest of the canonical books he only acknowledged ten epistles of Paul (excluding Hebrews and the Pastoral Epistles), to which he gave the name of *Apostolicon.* His opinions are to be learned mainly from Tertullian and Epiphanius, who undertook to refute them.

The Epistle to Diognetus is "one of the noblest and most impressive of early Christian apologies in style and treatment." It is addressed by an anonymous author to an educated Pagan in answer to his inquiries about Christianity. While certainly not the work of Justin Martyr (to whom it has sometimes been attributed), it probably dates from the second century. The only MS. containing it (of the thirteenth century) was destroyed in Strassburg in 1870 during the Franco-German War. It consists of twelve short chapters, but the last two are probably of a much later date, and bear traces of an Alexandrian origin.

Justin Martyr, a native of Samaria, of Greek descent, after having tried various forms of Greek philosophy, especially Platonism, was converted to Christianity and became its zealous advocate at Rome, Ephesus, and elsewhere. Of his numerous writings there have been preserved to us (besides a few fragments) two *Apologies* addressed to Roman Emperors in vindication of the Christian life, and a *Dialogue with Trypho,* a Jew, being the account of a discussion at Ephesus, in which Justin sought to prove that Jesus was the Christ. He wrote before the middle of the second century, and was martyred about 165 A.D.

Tatian, a native of Mesopotamia, was a teacher of rhetoric, well versed in Greek literature and philosophy. He came under the influence of Justin Martyr in Rome about 162 A.D., and became a zealous member of the Church; but on his return to the East, after the death of Justin, he fell into Gnosticism of a peculiar type, and was regarded as the father of the Encratites (ascetics). Among numerous other works he wrote an Apology under the name of an *Address to the Greeks,* which is still extant, and a kind of Harmony of the Four Gospels which he called *Diatessaron.*

Athenagoras, an Athenian philosopher of the school of Platonists, wrote an Apology (176 A.D.) strongly resembling that of Justin, and a treatise on the Resurrection, both of which are extant and exhibit considerable intellectual power.

Melito, Bishop of Sardis, a man of wide influence in Asia Minor, wrote on a great variety of subjects. Among his works (only fragments of which have come down to us) was an Apology addressed to Marcus Aurelius (177 A.D.), designed to avert the rising persecution by vindicating the character of the Christians.

Theophilus, Bishop of Antioch (171-184 A.D.), was a prolific writer; but the only undoubted work of his that has come down to us is his *Apologia ad Autolycum,* in three books, in which he bases his argument for Christianity largely on the Old Testament.

The **Muratorian Fragment**, discovered by Muratori in a MS. of the eighth century, in the Ambrosian Library at Milan (1730-1740 A.D.), contains a list of the canonical books. It is in very bad Latin, apparently a translation from the Greek, but copied from an older MS. that had been previously mutilated. It is usually assigned to about 170 A.D.

Lyons and Vienne, Letter from the Churches of to the Christians of Asia and Phrygia (177 A.D.), which has been preserved by Eusebius, tells the story of a dreadful local persecution, in which forty-eight Christians suffered martyrdom.

Irenæus, a native of Asia Minor, and a disciple of Polycarp, was appointed Bishop of Lyons 178 A.D. He had previously visited Rome as a delegate from the persecuted Church in Gaul, and had come into contact with many of the leading heretics. In order to counteract their teaching (especially that of Valentinus the Gnostic) he composed a *Refutation*, in five books, which has been preserved to us in a Latin translation, with fragments of the Greek and of a Syriac translation. It abounds in quotations from nearly all the books of the New Testament, and also embodies a number of traditions of "Elders"—men of a former generation, some of whom had been disciples of Apostles. Most of his other writings have perished.

Clement of Alexandria was head of the Catechetical School of Alexandria from 190 to 203 A.D., during which time he accomplished much literary work. His three chief writings that have come down to us are (1) his *Address to the Greeks*, designed to show the superiority of Christianity to all the religion and culture of heathenism ; (2) *The Tutor*, a text-book of Christian discipline ; (3) the *Miscellanies*, a kind of harmony of the truths of philosophy from a Christian point of view.

Tertullian (*circa* 160-230 A.D.), a native of Carthage, was a married presbyter of the Church, but in his later years a votary of Montanism ("the Irvingism of the second century"). He wrote both in Greek and Latin, but only his Latin works have been preserved to us, which are very

numerous and varied.   He was a keen and able contro-
versialist (with a strong anti-gnostic bent), and defended
Christianity against heathens, Jews, and heretics.

Hegesippus, an ecclesiastical writer of the second century,
of Jewish descent and a member of the Church at Jerusalem,
published (about 180 A.D.), five books of *Memorials*, fragments
of which have been preserved by Eusebius.   Hegesippus had
previously visited Rome (where he appears to have spent
many years), taking Corinth on the way, and making inquiry
as to the Apostolic tradition.   According to Eusebius, he
found "everywhere the same doctrine."

Clementine Homilies (in Greek) and **Recognitions** (in
a Latin translation by Rufinus) are based on the same original
(an account of Peter's discourses to the heathen), but are in
some respects widely different, the *Homilies* being strongly
Ebionite in doctrine, the *Recognitions* more adapted for the
use of the orthodox.   They consist largely of a romantic
story of the travels of Clement (the future Bishop of Rome)
in attendance on Peter, whose discourses he records ; and
they were evidently designed to exalt Peter as the apostle of
the Gentiles at the expense of Paul, who is covertly referred
to under the name of Simon Magus. The *Homilies* are
twenty in number, and are addressed to James, the head of
Jewish Christianity ; the *Recognitions* derive their name from
the hero's finding in succession his lost mother, brothers, and
father. In their present form, the compositions may be assigned
to the end of the second or beginning of the third century.

Hippolytus (170-235 A.D.), a hearer of Irenæus, and a
Roman ecclesiastic of great importance in his day, whether
as presbyter or bishop, wrote many books, of which the
principal extant is his *Refutation of all Heresies*.   Part of
this work, under the name of *Philosophoumena*, used to be
attributed to Origen, but in 1842 a MS. containing seven of
the ten books of which the work is composed was discovered
on Mount Athos, and it is now generally acknowledged to
have been written by Hippolytus.   Its chief value for us lies
in the account which it gives of the Gnostic heresies of the
second century, tracing them to heathen sources.   Hippolytus
was ultimately banished to the mines of Sardinia, where he
is believed to have perished.

Origen (186-254 A.D.), a pupil of Clement Alex. and a man of immense industry and learning, exerted a wide influence by his lectures in Alexandria, Jerusalem, Cæsarea, Athens, and elsewhere. He was a most voluminous writer on biblical, theological, and philosophical subjects. Eusebius tells us that he kept more than seven shorthand writers employed, besides as many copyists, and several female caligraphists. His chief work extant (besides Commentaries and Homilies in Latin translations) is his *Eight Books against Celsus*, in defence of Christianity. His life was one of struggle and hardship. In the Decian persecution he underwent torture, and died soon afterwards at Tyre.

Firmilian, Bishop of Cæsarea in Cappadocia (about 230-270 A.D.), was an intimate friend of Origen. His only writing extant is a letter to Cyprian, which has been preserved in the form of a Latin translation.

Cyprian, a wealthy teacher of rhetoric in Carthage, was converted 246 A.D., became bishop of his native city in 248 or 249, and suffered martyrdom 258 A.D. His extant works consist of controversial treatises and official letters.

Eusebius (260-339 A.D.), Bishop of Cæsarea, and friend of Constantine the Great, has been called the "Father of Church History," as Origen the "Father of Biblical Criticism." His *Ecclesiastical History*, in ten books, gives an account of the Christian Church down to 324 A.D. Although Eusebius himself seems to have been of a rather weak judgment, the facts and quotations with which his History teems make it a mine of wealth for the historian and the critic. Of his other works, the most valuable are his *Gospel Preparation* and *Gospel Demonstration*, both of an apologetic nature.

Athanasius (299-373 A.D.), Bishop of Alexandria, and the champion of orthodoxy in the great Arian Controversy, wrote numerous letters and treatises, chiefly of a doctrinal nature.

Cyril of Jerusalem (315-386 A.D.), appointed bishop of his native city in 351, left a large number of catechetical addresses, which are valuable for the information they yield regarding the doctrine and the ritual of the early Church.

Apostolic Constitutions, an ecclesiastical miscellany in eight books, not earlier (in its present form) than the middle of the fourth century.

Gregory Nazianzen (329-389 A.D.), son of a bishop of Nazianzus, was in his youth a fellow-student at Athens with Basil the Great and the Emperor Julian. At one time Archbishop of Constantinople, he was famous for learning and eloquence, and left an immense number of orations, epistles, and poems.

Basil the Great, born in Cæsarea (Cappadocia) in 330 A.D., succeeded Eusebius in the bishopric in 370, and died 379. A man of great elevation of character, he was the author of many works of a theological nature, still extant.

Gregory of Nyssa (332-395 A.D.), younger brother of Basil, held various positions in the Eastern Church, and was one of the most powerful defenders of the orthodox faith, in opposition to Arius and Apollinaris. His writings are numerous, and include both controversial and exegetical works.

Epiphanius, Bishop of Constantia (Salamis) in Cyprus (367 - 403 A.D.), published in 377 A.D. his chief work (*Panarium*), dealing with eighty different heresies. He was famous for his learning and piety, but was deficient in breadth of view, and his statements are often inaccurate. He was strongly opposed to the school of Origen.

Chrysostom (*golden-mouthed*) was born at Antioch in 347 A.D., appointed Patriarch of Constantinople in 397, and martyred 407 A.D. He was the greatest preacher of the Greek Church, and left many valuable writings, the most important of which are his *Homilies*.

Jerome or **Hieronymus** (341-420 A.D.), the greatest scholar of the Latin Church, and the translator of the Vulgate, left a variety of biblical and ecclesiastical works. In his later life he dwelt in a hermit's cell, near Bethlehem.

Augustine, born in Numidia in 354 A.D., was converted, after a stormy youth, by Ambrose of Milan in 386, and became Bishop of Hippo, in North Africa, about 396. He moulded the theology of his own and later times, and left numerous writings, the most famous of which are his *Confessions* and *City of God*. He died in 430, during the siege of Hippo by the Vandals.

APPENDIX B

UNDESIGNED COINCIDENCES IN THE GOSPELS (p. 19).

(For a fuller statement see Blunt's *Scriptural Coincidences*.)

(1) Cf. Matt. xiv. 1, and Luke ix. 7, with Luke viii. 3 (and Acts xiii. 1) for an explanation of Herod's having "*heard of all that was done*" and speaking "unto *his servants*" about Jesus—viz. that there were believers at Herod's court ("Joanna the wife of Chuza Herod's steward," and "Manaen, the foster-brother of Herod the tetrarch ").

(2) Cf. Matt. xiv. 19, 20 ; Mark vi. 39, 43 ; Luke ix. 17 ; John vi. 10, 13 ; with Matt. xv. 35, 37 ; Mark viii. 6, 8 (in the light of Matt. xvi. 9, 10) for a remarkable distinction carefully observed (1) between the two kinds of baskets (only discernible in the original, ($\delta\acute{\omega}\delta\epsilon\kappa\alpha$) $\kappa o\phi\acute{\imath}\nu ov\varsigma$ in the one case, ($\acute{\epsilon}\pi\tau\grave{a}$) $\sigma\pi\nu\rho\acute{\imath}\delta\alpha\varsigma$ in the other) ; (2) between " the grass " and "the ground " ; and (3) between " the men " and " the people."

(3) Cf. Matt. viii. 16 with Mark i. 21 and Luke iv. 31 (in the light of Matt. xii. 10) for an explanation of the fact that the sick were only brought to Jesus for healing "*when the even was come*"—viz. that it was the Sabbath day, during which it was considered by the Jews to be unlawful to heal.

(4) Cf. Matt. xii. 46 ; Mark vi. 3 ; Luke viii. 19 ; John ii. 12 ; xix. 25-27 (and Acts i. 13, 14)—all these passages concurring in giving the impression, although in an indirect manner, that Joseph was already dead.

(5) Cf. John xxi. 15 with Matt. xxvi. 31-33 and Mark xiv. 27-29—the two latter (which record Peter's boasts) supplying an explanation of the former passage, where "Jesus saith to Simon Peter, Simon, son of John, lovest thou me *more than these ?* "

(6) Cf. Matt. iv. 13 (" he came and dwelt in Capernaum ") with Luke iv. 23 and x. 15—with reference to *Capernaum* as a favoured scene of Christ's ministry.

(7) Cf. Matt. xxvi. 67, 68 ("Prophesy unto us, thou Christ : who is he that struck thee? ') with Luke xxii. 64— the latter explaining the former by the addition " *they blindfolded him* "—although evidently an independent narrative.

(8) Cf. Matt. xxvi. 65 (in the light of John v. 18, x. 33) with Luke xxiii. 2—the former referring to Christ's trial before the *Jewish Council* on a charge of *blasphemy*, the latter to His trial before *Pilate* on a charge of *sedition*, the accusation in each case corresponding to the tribunal.

(9) Cf. Matt. xxvi. 71 with John xviii. 16—the latter explaining indirectly how Peter should have been recognised in " *the porch* "—viz. because he " was standing at the door without " until " the other disciple, which was known unto the high-priest, went out and spake unto her that kept the door, and brought in Peter."

(10) Cf. Mark vi. 31 with John vi. 4 (" Now the passover . . . was at hand ")—the latter supplying an explanation of the great number of people in the neighbourhood at the time.

(11) Cf. John vi. 5, 8 with Luke ix. 10 and John i. 44, with reference to the connection of *Philip* and *Andrew* with *Bethsaida, in the neighbourhood of which the miracle was wrought.*

(12) Cf. John iii. 13, vi. 62, xx. 17 (where our Lord's Ascension is indirectly referred to) with the actual record of that event in Luke xxiv. 50-53.

LIST OF BOOKS ON THE SUBJECT

Westcott (Bishop), *Introduction to the Four Gospels.* 10s. 6d.

,,   *The Canon of the New Testament.* 10s. 6d.

,,   *On the Epistles of St. John.* 9s. 6d.

,,   *On the Epistle to the Hebrews.* 14s.

Dale (Dr.), *The Living Christ and the Four Gospels.* 6s.

Farrar (Dean), *The Messages of the Books*—Discourses and Notes on the New Testament. 14s.

Fraser (Dr. D.), *Synoptical Lectures.* 2 Vols. 15s.

Charteris (Prof.), *The New Testament Scriptures.* 7s. 6d.

,,   *Canonicity.* 18s.

Conybeare and Howson's *Life and Epistles of St. Paul.* 6s.

Godet (Dr.), *New Testament Studies.* 7s. 6d.

,,   *Studies on the Epistles.* 7s. 6d.

,,   *The Epistles of St. Paul.* 12s. 6d.

Dods (Prof. Marcus), *Introduction to the New Testament.* 2s. 6d.

Salmon (Prof.), *Introduction to the New Testament.* 9s.

Norton (Rev. A.), *Evidences of the Genuineness of the Gospel.* 7s. 6d.

Stanley (Dean), *The Epistle to the Corinthians.* With Critical Notes and Dissertations. 18s.

Lightfoot (Bishop), *Commentary on Galatians.* 12s.

,,   *Commentary on Colossians and Philemon.* 12s.

,,   *Commentary on Philippians.* 12s.

,,   *Biblical Essays.* 12s.

,,   *Notes on the Epistles of St. Paul.* 12s.

Findlay (Prof.), *The Epistles of the Apostle Paul.* 2s. 6d.

Matheson (Dr.), *The Spiritual Development of St. Paul.* 5s.

Sabatier (A.), *Paul. Sketch of Development of his Doctrine.* 7s. 6d.

Paley (Archdeacon), *Horæ Paulinæ.* 1s.

Blunt (Rev. J. J.), *Scripture Coincidences.* 6s.

Cambridge Bible for Schools and Colleges. 18 Vols. from 1s. tc
4s. 6d.

Expositor's Bible—on New Testament. 20 Vols. 7s. 6d. each.

Speaker's Commentary. Student's Edition. New Testament.
2 Vols. 7s. 6d. each.

Smyth (Paterson), *How we got our Bible.* 1s.

Alford (Dean), *How to Study the New Testament.* 3 Vols. 3s. 6d.
each

,,   *The Greek New Testament.* 4 Vols. £2.

Sanday (Prof.), *Authorship of the Fourth Gospel.* 8s. 6d.

Alexander (Bishop), *Leading Ideas of the Gospels.* 6s.

Gloag (Dr.), *Introduction to the Synoptic Gospels.* 7s. 6d.

,,   *Introduction to the Pauline Epistles.* 12s.

,,   *Introduction to the Catholic Epistles.* 10s. 6d.

,,   *Introduction to the Johannine Epistles.* 10s. 6d.

Reith (Dr.), *St. John's Gospel.* 4s. (Published in T. & T. Clark's
series of Bible-Class Handbooks.)

Thomson (Rev. Ed. A.), *The Four Evangelists.* 3s. 6d.

Jowett (Prof.), *Epistles of St. Paul to the Thessalonians, Galatians,
and Romans.* 2 Vols. 7s. 6d. each.

Weiss (Prof.), *Manual of Introduction to the New Testament.* 2 Vols.
7s. 6d. each.

Hort (Dr.), *Prolegomena to the Epistles of St. Paul to the Ephesians
and the Romans.* 6s.

International Critical Commentary—in course of publication.
12s. per vol.

Westcott and Hort, *Introduction to the New Testament in the
Original Greek.* 10s. 6d.

Scrivener (Dr.), *Introduction to the Criticism of the New Testament.*
2 Vols. 32s.

Hammond (C. E.), *Outlines of Textual Criticism.* 4s. 6d.

Warfield (Prof.), *Textual Criticism of the New Testament.* 2s. 6d.

THE END

A LIFE OF CHRIST FOR YOUNG PEOPLE.

THE STORY OF STORIES

By the Rev. R. C. GILLIE, M.A.

IN LARGE SQUARE CROWN 8vo, CONTAINING 32 PAGE ILLUS-
TRATIONS, AND HAVING AS A FRONTISPIECE LUINI'S
FAMOUS FRESCO, MARY AND JESUS AND THE INFANT JOHN,
REPRODUCED IN THE COLOURS OF THE ORIGINAL

PRICE **6/-** CLOTH, GILT TOP

ALSO TO BE HAD IN WHITE CLOTH, EXTRA GILT,
WITH GILT EDGES, PRICE **7/6**

THE AIM OF THE BOOK

is to provide a life of Christ which will be thoroughly attractive to children, and at the same time will present the incidents of the sacred story in such a fashion that nothing will need to be unlearned. An extravagant use of local colour and of the imagination has been avoided, but an actual and living person is vividly portrayed. Everything that would blur and confuse the picture has been avoided, and no attempt has been made to reproduce the whole of the material in the four Gospels. Only the most important incidents and sayings, and those which appeal most directly to the minds of children, have been selected. The hinge-points in the ministry have been emphasised, so that the book is not a collection of stories, but a connected narrative. At the same time the mysterious majesty of the central figure has been carefully preserved, but without the use of theological language.

SOME PRESS OPINIONS

"This beautiful volume is a life of Christ for the young, which is compiled with infinite judgment and infinite care."—*The Rock.*

"No clearer or more appealing story of Christ could be desired for placing in the hands of children as their first introduction to the Gospels."—*The Bookman.*

"The introduction is altogether admirable. The chapters headed 'What Jesus was like,' and 'The Land where Jesus lived,' and 'The People among whom Jesus lived,' are not only written in simple language that children will understand, but are so really descriptive, and even picturesque, that their parents will find pleasure and profit in the reading."—*The Daily News.*

"Mr. Gillie is a wise and tender guide for the lads and maids who will take his hand and let him lead them into the Holy of Holies—the Wonderful Life. The book is beautiful without as well as within."—*The Monthly Messenger.*

"We know of no 'Life of Christ' which we would more gladly put into a child's hand than this."—*The Sunday School Chronicle.*

A. & C. BLACK, SOHO SQUARE, LONDON.

THE NEW TESTAMENT AND ITS WRITERS

By the Rev. J. A. M'CLYMONT, D.D., Aberdeen.

New and Enlarged Edition. Specially adapted for the use of Teachers.
Demy 8vo, cloth, 288 pp. **Price 3s. 6d. net.**

"Mr. M'Clymont has prepared himself for his task by wide reading and minute study. Evidence of sound judgment and abundant information appears on every page."—*The British Weekly.*

"The work is one of much value. It displays wide scholarship and a thorough acquaintance with the subjects treated, and that ability for making difficult things plain which is so desirable and yet so rare."—*The Scotsman.*

In one volume, large crown 8vo, cloth, gilt top. **Price 7s. 6d.**

THE HISTORY OF THE
REFORMATION OF RELIGION
WITHIN THE REALM OF SCOTLAND

WRITTEN BY

JOHN KNOX

EDITED FOR POPULAR USE BY

C. J. GUTHRIE, Q.C.

SECOND EDITION

WITH NOTES, SUMMARY, GLOSSARY, INDEX, AND FIFTY-SIX ILLUSTRATIONS

"The task is one which Carlyle desired to see accomplished nearly thirty years ago, when he wrote in one of the least known of his works : 'It is really a loss to English, and even to universal literature, that Knox's hasty and strangely interesting, impressive, and peculiar book . . . has not been rendered far more extensively legible to serious mankind at large than is hitherto the case.' It will be interesting to see if Mr. Guthrie's labour can restore John Knox's 'History' to the place of honour it once held, but seems long to have lost, among Scottish classics."—*Glasgow Herald.*

"Mr. Guthrie is to be heartily congratulated on this attempt to popularise Knox's 'History,' which has never before been presented in such an attractive form. . . . And while a mere acquaintance with this edition will doubtless bring delight to many readers who would never have tackled the work in a less pleasing guise, it may induce some of them to study it seriously in that archaic and genuine form for the elucidation of which David Laing did so much."—*D. HAY FLEMING in The Bookman.*

A. & C. BLACK, SOHO SQUARE, LONDON.